Advance Praise

"*Welcoming All That We Are* starts with a quote by Leymah Gbowee: '*When women gather, great things happen.*' This book offers 52 exercises for any women's group to support creating those great things, developing relationships, and delving into spirituality in a safe, collective way. If you have ever wanted to start a group or wish to deepen the activities of the group you already have, this book is a great tool to bring women together."
~**Sharon Salzberg,** author of *Lovingkindness* and *Real Happiness*

"For the past thirty years, we have consulted the African oracles for guidance on how to live in harmony with nature and each other. And we are consistently advised to 'return to the ways of our ancestors, to respect the elders and care for the children and most importantly to let the voices of the women be heard.' In this book, *Welcoming All That We Are*, the voices of three generations of women can be heard encouraging us to heal, calling us into kinship, and inspiring us to create an empowered and beautiful world. Surely the ancestors are pleased."
~**Yeye Luisah Teish,** storyteller-activist, spiritual counselor, and author of *Jambalaya, the Natural Woman's Book of Personal Charms and Practical Rituals*

"Ever wanted to start a life-changing women's group but have no idea how to go about it? This is your ultimate resource. Full of wisdom, beauty, practical tips and concrete exercises, this book is a treasure trove of inspiration for tapping into the divine feminine."
~**Kristin Neff,** Author of *Fierce Self-Compassion: How Women Can Harness Kindness to Speak Up, Claim Their Power and Thrive*

"It's time to gather the wisdom, heart and compassionate action of women all over the world. If you've been feeling this calling, *Welcoming All That We Are* is essential reading to guide your gathering journey. Grounded in ancient wisdom across cultures, and more relevant today than ever, *Welcoming All that We Are* offers practical tools from authentic feminine leaders to help empower your community."

~**Shamini Jain,** Founder & CEO, Consciousness and Healing Initiative, author of *Healing Ourselves: Biofield Science and the Future of Health*

"At a time when it can feel like the world is spinning out of control, it's so important to find comfort and support with others—and this beautiful practical book shows many ways to do this. Three generations of women—a therapist, a researcher, and an artist—have authored this guide, which provides detailed instructions for simple, yet wonderful activities timed with the four seasons. What a gift! Written from the heart while grounded in the science of positive change, this book fills a unique need and deserves to become a classic."

~ **Rick Hanson, Ph.D.,** author of *Resilient: How to Grow an Unshakable Core of Calm, Strength, and Happiness*

"Written and illustrated by three generations, *Welcoming All That We Are* is a wonderful collection of women's group exercises that reflects the years of experience of the authors."

~**Shauna Shapiro, PhD,** Professor, author of Good *Morning, I Love You: Mindfulness and Self-Compassion Practices to Rewire Your Brain for Calm, Clarity, and Joy*

"As we navigate the next few decades on this planet women are going to need each other's support, imagination, joy, insight, and presence more than ever. This book, birthed by a group of remarkable women, will help you create your own safe haven to become the you this planet needs. I have witnessed the magic of women's groups to birth new worlds and with this book, these worlds will be more beautiful than we could possibly imagine. Don't know how to start your own women's group? Or bring your group to the next level? This remarkable book, written by a group of intergenerational women, will show you how. Each page is a gift to help you and your sisters create the conditions conducive to grace-filled and lasting transformation."

~**Bristol Baughan,** Emmy-award winning filmmaker, founder of Inner Astronauts

"How wonderful! This marvelous book is just what we need in a time when women coming together is so essential. In our modern world, women have been separated into individual households and are often cut off from the ancient power of living and working together. As we awaken to the Arising Energy of the Feminine, women gathering in circle is vital for our own well being, and for our deepening service to the world. Twenty-five years ago, I shared with the world a native perspective on moon lodges and menstrual mysteries for personal wellness, deepening spirituality, and unique service to the world; yet many groups fell apart for lack of understanding what they could do in these precious circles. Now these three beautiful women coming together to offer us a way forward is timely, precious and important. May you have the joy of participating in a nurturing circle of women!!"

~ **Brooke Medicine Eagle**, author of *Buffalo Woman Comes Singing*, *The Last Ghost Dance*, and the Power and Beauty Wisdom Series course for empowering women: www.medicineeagle.com

Welcoming All That We Are

Kirk House Publishers

Welcoming All That We Are

52 Activities for Women's Groups

by

Billie Rogers, MA, MFT
Cassandra Vieten, PhD
Illustrated by Indigo Vieten

Paperback ISBN: 9781952976353
LCCN: 2021925283

Illustrated by Indigo Vieten

Cover and interior design by Ann Aubitz

First Printing: February 2022

First Edition

Published by Kirk House Publishers
1250 E 115th Street
Burnsville, MN 55337
Kirkhousepublishers.com
612-781-2815

Dedicated to

Angeles Arrien
(1940 - 2014)
and
Nancee Redmond
(1940 - 2005)
mentors and friends who illuminated the path
and led the way.

and

Dennis E. Smith, exemplary husband, father, and grandfather
who teaches us every day what it means
to love unconditionally.

Table of Contents

AUTUMN 97

WINTER 131

Preface

Billie

When my daughter Cassi said, *Mom, we should write a book together. We could write about our experiences leading women's groups,* I felt the physical sensation I have when an important threshold appears in front of me. I felt the cells in my body whirl around, the signal I recognize and know not to ignore that inspires me to say yes to a life-changing and enriching challenge.

I've led many different kinds of support groups for 40 years in my roles as a teacher, educational counselor, and Marriage and Family Therapist. I have led mostly women's groups for the past 30. I am delighted to share my personal history leading groups with my daughter and my artist granddaughter, Indigo, as we collaborate on a book that we believe will be helpful to other women.

I was blessed to have several life-enhancing mentors and teachers. The wisdom and gifts of two in particular, Angeles Arrien and Nancee Redmond, are reflected in this book. Participating in their groups was like being in multiple-year master classes. The professional, collaborative, and personal relationships we shared encourage me to carry on some of their work, especially after both Nancee and Angeles died before their time.

In 1995 Nancee announced the birth of a two-year women's program she called *Thiasos: Women Who Are Attentive to the Mystery.* It was the culmination of a dream she had been carrying for a long time, a dream about a community of women coming together to deepen their connection to each other and to their creative fire. I was one of those women, and for the next six years I was in three separate *Thiasos* groups, each of whom created a deeply connected community, bonded together by our longing to grow, be authentic, and make the unconscious conscious.

In each *Thiasos*, at the end of two years of transformational weekends and monthly meetings focusing on the Divine Feminine and engaging in spiritual practices from many traditions, we traveled together on two-week pilgrimages to sacred places in France, culminating with a visit to the Black Madonna in Rocamadour. Over the years, we shared the deep work and leadership during our pilgrimages.

After Nancee passed away, we women kept our connection, and a group of us have met in our own *Thiasos* for 20 years, honoring departing women and thoughtfully welcoming new members over the years. We share leadership, and use poetry, myths, music, storytelling, and rituals that enrich our time together. We have created a container where we can be genuine and joyful and carry each other through difficult times.

As I added to my skills as a Counselor and Marriage and Family Therapist, Nancee, first as my teacher and later as a colleague, inspired my interest in Jungian psychology and introduced many women's spirituality books and practices into my life.

Angeles Arrien's intensive workshops and books, including *The Four-Fold Way: Walking the Paths of the Warrior, Teacher, Healer and Visionary* and *The Second Half of Life,* among many others in our Recommended Reading, have been integral to my work leading women's groups. I am happy that Cassi had the opportunity to have Angie as a teacher and colleague.

Whether as a leader or group member, I strive to model the four universal principles Angie taught in *The Four-Fold Way* workshops and book. These are: 1) Show up, or choose to be present; 2) Pay attention to what has heart and meaning; 3) Tell the truth without blame or judgment; and 4) Be open to outcome, not attached to outcome. I recommend you pick up a copy of the book, which explores the theory and practice of these four *ways of being* that have helped me become a more effective leader and mentor.

While most of my group work has been with women, I'm deeply grateful that my very supportive husband also had the opportunity to attend *The Four-Fold Way* training, and also became friends with Angeles. As our enthusiastic travel planner, he has helped make it possible for us to visit scores of women's sacred sites in Europe, Great Britain, and Ireland.

When I was new to leading groups, many other books helped me understand and become better at the work I was doing. Christina Baldwin's how-to book, *Calling the Circle: The First and Future Culture,* provided a detailed guide about forming and leading groups, including their challenges, in various settings. Jean Shinoda Bolen's workshops and books, including *The Millionth Circle: How to Change Ourselves and the World* and *Crossing to Avalon,* inspired me to heed the call to lead more women's groups during and after I completed my career in educational settings.

I added to my knowledge and skills by participating in many workshops led by Angeles and Nancee, as well as Marion Woodman, Brooke Medicine Eagle, Merlin Stone, Maureen Murdock, Layne Redmond, Matthew Fox, and many others. I participated in healing-through-poetry workshops with David Whyte and John Fox, and for two years in a Jungian dreamwork group led by Sharon Smith.

Today, my ongoing transformational work with women's groups helps me remember what we do together is *big* work. It is valuable work. We become more insightful and aware of our bodies' wisdom, and we always have a place to share the joyful and challenging events and transitions in our lives. It allows us to feel the rhythm and flow of our lives, the ups and downs. It helps us embody feminine attributes that create balance in our lives, and experience mystery and magic in the rituals we create together.

I have learned that rationality *by itself* does not equal wisdom. I learned to listen for and rely on the voice of inner wisdom instead of outer approval, and to listen to what my body tells me when my mind is unsettled. When I was a young woman, repressing spontaniety and playfulness, neglecting self-care, and rigid attention to duty were prevalent in my life. Letting go of those restrictions (and endless lists of pros and cons) allowed me to open doors that led to more joyful, numinous, and sacred experiences.

Women thrive in a setting where we can share our dreams and our stories. One night when my granddaughter Indigo and I were cuddled up at bedtime she said, *Grambie, would you read me a story?* I said, *I can't read, Indi.*

It's dark. She said, *No, I mean read me one from inside your head.* That's where our stories are; they're inside our heads and our hearts, waiting to be claimed.

Cassandra

The importance of women's groups in my life ranks just below food, water, shelter, and family. I would no more live without a women's group in my life than I would live without books, music, and love. My women's groups have been a crucial part of my personal and spiritual journey. My mother was my role model for prioritizing women's groups, having women's empowerment and peace-building groups in our living room since I was a kid, and I've been lucky to follow in her footsteps.

My mom calls me now and then and asks, *What's a good idea for my women's group this weekend?* It's always been a great conversation, and despite our experience working with women's groups, sometimes we are stumped. Last year when the holidays rolled around, I thought, *I'll get my mom a book of ideas for women's groups*, thinking there would be tons of them out there. I was surprised to find there were very few! I called her and said, *Hey, Mom! We should write a book about women's groups.* That has turned out to be a much larger gift to us than I could have imagined. Including my daughter Indigo's illustrations made it even more special for us.

I believe my desire to gather in women's circles is both hard-wired and learned. For millennia women have gathered during hunting, food preparation, toolmaking, gathering, creating, and menses or moon times. In cultures where women are oppressed, we have created a culture within a culture, behind closed doors. In quilting circles, in covens, in social justice action, in suffrage, in pregnancy, in healthcare—women have always gathered for mutual support, empowerment, safety, and growth.

Only very recently in our evolutionary timeline has the single woman in a nuclear family, essentially isolated, working inside and outside the home, been the norm, and still it is not in many cultures. But women working alone, cooking alone, creating in isolation, or parenting without a village feels biologically and socially unnatural. Women have always circled up to do these things. I feel naturally attracted to participating in and leading women's groups from a place deep in my bones, perhaps because it is likely evolutionarily adaptive.

My love of women's groups, as you can tell from my mom's introduction above, is also a gift of my upbringing. Soon after my parents' divorce when I was nine, I saw my mother blossom into a massive amount of transformational work, at the core of which was women gathering in art, music, ritual, and personal growth. As she trained to be a Jungian-inspired feminist psychologist, and women began to gather in our living room, I witnessed the healing, supportive, and transformative power of women's groups.

In my early clinical work, I led multiple groups of women facing recovery from substance dependence, domestic violence, and histories of trauma. In my doctoral psychology program at the California Institute of Integral Studies, I chose a concentration in women's spirituality, immersing myself in the work of Jean Shinoda Bolen, Starhawk, Luisah Teish, Angeles Arrien, Clarissa Pinkola Estes, Vendana Shiva, Joanna Macy, Frances Vaughan, Charlene Spretnak, Mara Lynn Keller, and many more. I devoured the writing of Barbara Kingsolver, Isabel Allende, Toni Morrison, Ursula K. LeGuin, Alice Walker, Zora Neale Thurston, Louise Erdrich, Amy Tan, and many others. Later as I became focused on practicing and studying mindfulness as a pathway to emotional balance, behavioral health, and awakening, I learned from Sylvia Boorstein, Sharon Salzberg, Pema Chodron, Joan Halifax, and many others.

In multiple women's retreats, classes, workshops, groups, and informal gatherings, the value of women's groups has become a central part of my personal and professional life. For the last ten years, my women's group has been the WOW MOMS—Women of Wisdom, or Women of Wonder, we can never quite remember which. We've been through so much together—peak life experiences, cancer, promotions, pets, houses, divorce, graduations, alcoholism and recovery, books published, jobs gained, lost, and quit, kids winning awards, going to prom, graduating, getting into college, as well as being bullied, stalked, and hospitalized, and even the sudden loss of one of our children. The WOW has been our touchstone, our anchor, our compass, and our accountability partners through it all.

Co-ed group experiences and dozens of amazing men have played a large part in my life's journey, and I would not ever want to exclude the masculine from my world. My father, stepdad, partner, and male teachers and mentors have supported me, lifted me up, and taught me that women are beautiful, respected, brilliant, and sacred, and can do anything we set our minds to. However, there is something unique and magical that happens when women come together with intention. I'm excited, humbled, and honored to share the art of gathering women with you, and hope it helps you create a safe and brave space for women to gather in your own life.

***

Many of you already know the importance of women's groups and circles; we use these terms interchangeably. Some of you may be new to them, or new to being in a leadership role. And some of you have more experience than we do participating in and leading women's groups. We are happy, honored, and humbled to pass along to you what we have learned about creating strong, sustainable women's groups.

Introduction

When women gather, great things will happen.
~Leymah Gbowee, Nobel Laureate

When women come together, unique and powerful magic happens. We gather to tell the truth about our lives, to be authentic with one another, to sing, to vision, to drum, to dance, to make art, to organize, to cry, to recover and heal, to raise our voices, to make good trouble, to solve problems, to innovate, to lead, to mourn, to weave a blanket, or build a new world.

For millennia women have gathered in circles, in council and boardrooms, around cook pots and quilts, as royals and as slaves, in public and in secret, around fires and funeral pyres, during menses and menopause, as maidens, mothers, and elders, in PTAs and carpools, in politics and protests, at churches and synagogues, temples and shrines, mosques and kivas, among standing stones, and in meadows. Everywhere women are, they find a way to gather.

Why is it important for women to come together? In a world where women's voices have too often been silenced, diminished, invalidated, punished, ridiculed, and more, we need places where we can be ourselves without editing, and without fear of retribution. In societies and communities where women are honored and elevated, we still need places to gain inspiration and courage, where we can be genuine and welcomed for ALL that we are.

We need spaces where women's ways of inner knowing and intuition are valued, where we can experiment with creative spiritual and secular practices, where we can share our mistakes and victories and learn from each other's life experiences.

It can be difficult for women in today's world to find the natural opportunities to gather that were built in for previous generations. Fewer women attend organized religious services, more women work outside of the home, and families and often friends live in different cities. The sheer volume of activity and information overload that make up many modern women's lives means that spending dedicated meaningful time with other women can require that we formally set aside time for a women's group. If you are surrounded by women who are family and friends, it can be even *more* helpful to commit to a chosen group of women who meet regularly.

What Are Women's Groups?

The power of women coming together is multiplied when we meet with structure and shared intention. When we use the terms *women's group* or *women's circle* in this book, we mean a group of women who have decided to meet regularly to cultivate personal and/or spiritual growth. You might meet for one to three hours weekly or monthly, every full or new moon, or a half-day to a full day quarterly or biannually. You may already have a structured women's group as part of a spiritual community or religious organization, with a selected group of friends or colleagues, at a healthcare or treatment center, or at a community service organization. Your group may have shared circumstances or interests, such as surviving cancer or a commitment to environmental regeneration.

For those who don't have a structured women's group, you can join one, or start one by considering women who bring out the best in you and asking them if they would like to meet regularly. It might help to send them this book, or another book on women's groups from our Recommended Readings at the end of this book.

This Introduction gives you tips for starting or strengthening a women's group. The remainder of the book provides 52 activities with step-by-step guidelines and suggested resources that your women's group can use when you meet or modify in ways that work for your particular group.

What Can Women's Groups Offer?

A women's group can be an oasis, a place where we tend the gardens of our inner lives, find deeper parts of ourselves, and experience renewal.

They are where we can be unabashedly joyful, share difficulties, or deeply grieve. They can be challenging and can ask us to be brave. Many of us joined our first group because we needed to heal or were searching for more real happiness in our lives. We weren't content to simply be content.

Creative intimacy grows in women's groups. They foster deep levels of trust, commitment, compassion, equality, and healing. In women's groups, we can be heard and respected as equals. We can let down our defenses and be ourselves. When we hear things that strongly resonate with us, it helps us find deeper meaning in our own lives.

Through guided imagery and exploring the archetypal patterns in our lives, we can connect to female ancestors and to the Divine Feminine. We celebrate our bodies by moving, and we connect with the healing powers of the elements of air, fire, water, and earth. We draw inspiration from the movement of summer into autumn, or winter to spring. Each season evokes feelings and memories, and the cycles of our lives. Celebrating the four seasons encourages us to embrace the darkness and the light, the letting go and welcoming in. We create rituals to mark seasonal passages and other special transitions.

We learn that self-knowledge is in our own interest. We become more honest with others and ourselves. We look at harmful patterns, and we discover more satisfying ways of thinking and being. We learn self-care is essential. We become more comfortable living in "the land of I-don't-know" and allowing events to unfold as they will. We learn the value of setting intentions that guide us toward where and how we want to spend our time to bring more meaning into our lives. We become more responsive and less reactive when unexpected crises appear.

Some quotes from our women's group members say it best:

- *I feel the history, story, and power of those who have gathered in circles before me, and I am lifted, sustained, affirmed, and challenged by their power, witness, and courage.*
- *Not a meeting goes by without laughter, wide-eyed insights, and spirits being lifted.*

- *I feel something larger enfolding us, holding us, as we speak, listen, honor, and love.*

- *I am opened through my sisters to new ways of seeing my life, new perspectives on the mundane.*

- *We see ourselves in each other and can laugh and love what we see in those reflections.*

- *My life is fuller because of having witnesses to my wonderings and wanderings.*

- *I can bring all that I am, even if what I am is broken at the time. I have a safe place to search for what I want and need to be in balance and to honor the cycles of my life.*

- *We come together to weave the threads of our lives, the cycles of joys and sorrows, and the connection that serves us collectively and individually.*

- *We play with art and music and tell old and new stories; our own stories link us to the ancient ones and each other.*

- *I learn that calling forth feminine wisdom and energy not only honors those of us in the circle, but also serves the greater good out in the world.*

- *We are attentive to different views and perspectives, the light and dark aspects of who we are, and when the trickster appears, we smile at her.*

- *We call on fair witnesses to provide a container to hold all that we are, to honor our commitment to speak the truth, and to learn and grow together.*

- *I practice authentic presence: honesty, trust, openness, respect, and vulnerability. I become reacquainted with my inner child, and relish playing with her.*

- *We share creative and transformational processes, and always discover deeper levels of self-knowledge.*

- *We share music, poetry, dance, songs, and stories. We celebrate life's transitions.*

- *I give and receive help in challenging times and recognize how vital it is to pass along our gifts within our circle.*

- *We retreat from the everyday world. We help each other slow down and luxuriate in silence as we listen to our inner wisdom.*

- *I practice holding my place in the circle through honest sharing and fair witnessing.*
- *We attend to the seasons' natural rhythms, knowing that we are not separate from nature but part of a deep natural dance.*
- *We hold each other in our hearts through all of our life journeys.*
- *I attend to the mysteries as women have done for many centuries, through creative practices that bring forth what has been lost.*
- *I find a womb of sorts, away from the daily world, that allows me intentional time and space to grow more fully into what my soul needs to thrive.*
- *We have a space to reflect and grow, to let go, and to practice and express gratitude.*
- *We learn again and again that when we share our collective memories, values, and desires, we are more prepared for whatever happens in the months to come. I am reminded of the words, love, and wisdom of our circle members, and my life is richer because of them.*

As women, we often intuitively know what we need to do about difficult situations or what we need to change to move forward, but we may feel frozen. We are typically conditioned to push our own needs aside and nurture others. In our women's groups, we can create a space entirely separate from the noise of societal expectations, reveal our true desires and needs, and be supported in pursuing them.

In a world where women are increasingly taking the lead, and outdated male-dominated hierarchies are being called out and crumbling, it has never been more important for women to come together with intention. Many of our mentors who introduced us to the power of women's groups taught that when a critical number of groups of women form, the world will change, and the balance between feminine and masculine energy will become a new norm.

Building a Sturdy Women's Group

The benefits of women's groups rely on building a strong container of safety and trust. Here we provide some of the core elements of women's groups that lead to greater support, honesty, safety, growth, empowerment, and lasting connection. These can be introduced to groups just beginning, or those that have been going strong for a while but need to be renewed, are adding new members, or want to connect at a deeper level.

Types of Groups

Leader-led and Leaderless Groups. Some women's groups have designated leaders, such as a counselor, retreat leader, or clergy member. In these groups, the leader facilitates most of the activities and may intervene if shared agreements are not honored.

Most women's groups are nonhierarchical, with all members taking collective responsibility for the group process. A model that works very well is to rotate leadership, where each woman takes a turn leading a meeting. The group offers a safe place for new members to stretch and grow. See our website for an example of this model.

Another option is for women to come together without a leader and follow the activity guidelines together. This works best when the group has been meeting for a while, has established trust, and can regulate itself. It helps to use more structures, such as timers, in a group without a facilitator.

Committed vs. Drop-In or Rotating Membership Groups. In some groups, commitment to the group is essential. Because a women's group is not a casual meeting, asking women to make attendance a priority creates an intentional community, a sisterhood of meaningful relationships. Not everyone will be able to be present at every single meeting, but a commitment to the group makes it more valuable to everyone. When commitment levels are not clear, it can be difficult to resolve the issues in the group.

In other groups, for example women's groups in a treatment facility, members may rotate in and out. New members will join, and others will leave. This does not prevent a powerful group experience but can require a stronger hand in facilitation. Leaders can make sure certain rituals are always followed, such as a particular reading at the beginning and end of each meeting. Leaders might maintain roles in the group that stay the same even when members change, such as timekeeper or note-taker. When done well, even if members completely replace themselves every several sessions, a certain spirit of the group can remain and be a through-line no matter how often members rotate.

Circling Up

It is ideal for women's groups to **meet in a circle**. For millennia, women have come together in circles. Circles allow us to share leadership or allow leadership without hierarchy. We circle up to be able to see one another, to hold hands, to share food and gifts, to honor the four directions and the center that connects us all.

The circle is a universal symbol across cultures. For example, in early Celtic times people lived in circular houses and danced at stone circles built by the first inhabitants of their lands. The Celtic cross, still seen in churchyards, town centers, and at crossroads, is a cross within a circle, symbolizing the oneness of all creation. Sharing wisdom in circles has been part of cultures around the world throughout humankind's history. Circle gatherings have taken place to celebrate joyful times, commemorate mournful occasions, and share the inevitable difficulties in life.

If your group location allows it, take the time to arrange the group in a circle. It reduces outside distractions and keeps the focus on each other. In Billie's women's group, a low table serves as an "altar" or symbolic hearth in the center of the circle, with a candle, flowers or greenery, and items related to the meeting's theme or the season.

Setting Intentions

Whether a group is just beginning or entering a new chapter, setting clear, honest intentions is key to creating a strong group. Even if the group has a stated purpose, such as a book study group, a women's spirituality group, or simply supporting one another, setting and sharing explicit intentions is important to create coherence and make sure people are on the same page.

An easy way to do this is to ask each woman in the group to take five minutes to journal about what intentions she holds for the group. Journal prompts could be: *What do you hope happens for you and others because of being in this group?* or *What attitudes, knowledge, and skills do you commit to bringing to this group?* At the end of the writing period, these intentions can be written on a whiteboard or flip chart, or one person can be a scribe, combining similar intentions. Members can discuss and revise any intentions people are not comfortable with. The goal is to end up with a list of shared intentions, like the following example.

We want to encourage a group where we:

- practice authentic presence that invites honesty, trust, openness, respect, and vulnerability;
- experience rituals that honor sacred space and the sacred feminine;
- share creative skills in transformational processes;
- discover deeper levels of self-knowledge and self-acceptance;
- celebrate life's transitions;
- give and receive help with problems;
- build a group of sisters of the heart;
- share our exceptional teachers' gifts;
- enjoy music, poetry, dance, and visual arts; and
- remember how valuable group work is.

Creating Shared Agreements

Shared Agreements have a different purpose than Setting Intentions. Shared Agreements create a safe and protected space where people can be brave and vulnerable, share what they hold sacred, and be open and honest. Women's groups are different from casual meetings and conversations. It is necessary to agree on how members will interact and speak.

Agreements provide safety for participants and provide consistency when leadership rotates, or members drop in.

A strongly recommended Shared Agreement is to *maintain confidentiality*. Trust in each other is vital. Everyone must feel safe both in and out of the group, knowing nothing shared in the group will be disclosed to others.

One form of confidentiality is obvious—agreeing not to share what you hear in the group with people outside of the group, even if you think they don't know anyone in the group. This applies even with your spouse, or very best friends. Exceptions to this are if you think a group member could be a danger to themselves or others, or if child or elder abuse is occurring. In that case, you are not breaking the confidentiality agreement if you notify the authorities. Ideally, you can support the person to do so herself.

Confidentiality has more subtle aspects, too, such as being cautious about where and when you discuss vulnerable information, even with other group members. It is jarring to be in a social situation with another group member and have her bring up a sensitive topic you shared in a group. It is also hurtful to learn other members were talking to each other outside of the group about what you shared in confidence, in sacred space. A good rule is: *What you hear here, who you see here, stays here when you leave here.*

Most groups agree **not to give unsolicited advice** or get into problem-solving mode unless the person specifically requests it. This practice serves us well in any situation but is essential in women's groups. Without intending to, one advice-giver can do grave damage to the group. For example, in one of our groups a woman mentioned that improving her physical health was an important goal for her. A well-intentioned member of the group began to offer unsolicited advice about intermittent fasting and a low-carb diet. This triggered memories of life-long criticism from others in the woman who was sharing, who flushed with shame and closed down, eventually withdrawing from the group. When unconscious projections are triggered, old wounds are revisited.

It is helpful for the group to explicitly agree to **practice attentive listening.** The group agrees to support each woman to access *her own* inner wisdom. Interruptions, questions, or crosstalk can distract the woman who is sharing and can lead her in an unhelpful direction. In new or large groups, passing a "talking stick" can provide structure and give the holder the chance to speak without interruptions. Bearing witness to another's story takes focus and deep listening. Empathy rather than judgment is required to listen attentively. If something is unclear *after* someone has finished sharing, a member can seek permission to request clarification, asking *Can I ask a clarifying question?* or *Can I reflect on what you've shared?* or *How can we support you?*

Sharing Time

It is important to make clear how long each group session will last, and how much time women will have for activities or sharing. Even in the most aware groups, dominant voices can crowd out more introverted ones, and sharing time can get increasingly long as the group goes from person to person. This seems to be a law of nature! We suggest holding boundaries about the amount of time each person has to share, whether in the full group, a small group, or a dyad.

In Cassi's women's group that has been meeting for years, we still set a timer for sharing. This might seem overly rigid or formal, but it has been key to making our group successful. We make an exception if a woman is in crisis or has a breakdown/breakthrough. For groups with more than six to eight women, we advise breaking up into dyads or triads for parts of the activities.

In our groups, **anyone can choose not to share at any time.** The group leader may ask if anyone who passed would like to speak after the others have finished. One of the leader's most important responsibilities is to make sure everyone's voice is heard.

Do More, Discuss Less

We recommend groups include no more than one-third (and often less) instruction, lectures, or spoken guidance. Our heartfelt suggestion is to spend less time yakking about the activities or concepts, and more time experiencing, doing, or being. At least one-third of the time should be spent in experiential activity, whether writing, creating art, meditating, or moving. A final one-third can be spent on discussion and sharing. You'll notice most of our Step-by-Step Guidelines generally follow this *rule of thirds* recommendation.

Even when activities are more psychological, when possible include poetry, music, visual art, or movement to enhance the experiential process. These let us slow down and drop into a space that opens us up and leads us toward a path to greater consciousness and insight.

You may choose to include simple rituals in group work, e.g., passing around a coin and infusing it with a wish for a group member who is leaving, or burning papers on which members have written something they want to let go of. Some of them will require a bit of preparation.

Opening and Closing the Circle

While our step-by-step guidelines for each activity do not explicitly say to *open the circle* and *close the circle*, we *strongly recommend* that you do. It is very helpful to open the circle each time you meet by creating a purposeful, intentional space for the group to take place. You could say out loud when the meeting is beginning, remind the group to turn off/put away mobile devices, dial down the chatting or small talk, and perhaps invoke the intentions and shared agreements for the group. In the first several meetings you might read your shared agreements out loud. In the following sessions you could say something like *Bringing to mind the intentions and shared agreements we have for this group* . . . without reading them out loud.

Later it can be as simple as saying *Ok, let's get started,* followed by ringing a bell, burning some sage, lighting a candle, saying a prayer, sharing a brief meditation or moment of silence, reading a poem, or listening to a song. It's a way of gathering everyone's attention and intention, just like you might gather the ingredients for a nourishing stew or the supplies you need to create a work of art. When the meeting is over, you might close the circle by blowing out candles, playing a song, resonating by holding hands and sharing the energy created during the group, reading a poem, or asking members to share what they appreciated about the experience. Suggestions for music, poetry, and other resources are included in the guidelines for each activity, and we encourage you to find your own.

Anticipating Bumps

It is not unusual for women's groups to have a few bumpy sessions before they find their groove. Remember every group will have members with different abilities and backgrounds, and their history of group experiences may vary widely, especially in groups where new members are added from time to time. Some will need to be gently reminded of the shared agreement—to share speaking time, not give unsolicited advice, or to show up on time. These are not problems, and in fact can be opportunities for groups to bond and clarify their shared agreements.

Tensions are to be expected, and with respect and commitment can strengthen the group. In Cassi's women's group, some members wanted to choose a monthly time to meet that did not change and others wanted to find a time each month when most people could make it. The tension between these two options made it so some people could not attend who wanted to, and others missed a few sessions, making women who had cleared their schedule for the sessions feel like they were more committed. It took a while, but everyone agreed to meet on the third Friday morning of the month, and to commit to keeping that time sacred as much as humanly possible. This has worked very well for years now, and the members learned a lot about themselves and each other in the process.

Honoring Cultures and Identities

Some of our book's activities borrow from cultures and identities that are not our own. Highlighting others' cultures or ancestral wisdom can be complex. Cultural appropriation, or inappropriately adopting elements of another culture or identity without acknowledgment, can be particularly disrespectful when aspects of the culture are trivialized, oversimplified, or used frivolously. When we share terminology, rituals, music, art, poetry, or ceremonies from others' cultures, we do so with the desire and commitment to understand, appreciate, honor, and learn from their perspectives and their wisdom.

Inclusivity

If you value inclusivity, welcoming women from all backgrounds, belief systems, and walks of life, we recommend that you make an explicit commitment to being inclusive by putting it in writing, saying it out loud, and being as complete, authentic, and enthusiastic in your welcome as possible. It may not be enough to assume that women with marginalized or minority identities will know that they are welcome, or that your group will welcome all women. For most underrepresented women, being welcomed into groups cannot be taken for granted.

In our groups and women's workshops, we make it a point to say out loud that we not only welcome but honor and appreciate women from a range of incomes, who have a range of body sizes, women of color, and people who identify as women but may not have been born with female anatomy. We welcome women of different cultures, ethnicities, and races that are traditionally underrepresented in our society—lesbian, bisexual, transgender women and those who identify as nonbinary, women who are across the political spectrum, women from various (or no) religions or spiritualities, and who have no children or many children.

You might decide that your women's group *does* have a focus that *by definition* excludes some women—not out of discrimination or thoughtlessness, but due to the focus or goals of the women in the group. You may have a mothers' group, or a Christian women's group, a meditation group, a group whose focus is on healthy nutrition and exercise, a philanthropy group, or a Latina women business leaders' group. It's important to explicitly state out loud and in writing about the group's focus upfront.

Conclusion

This book includes 52 activities for women's groups that are easy to access and implement. Although some groups meet monthly, we provide enough guidance for a yearlong weekly group. There are contemplative, celebratory, and transformative wisdom practices for your groups who meet in living rooms, book clubs, leadership programs, community centers, churches and spiritual communities, camps and after-school programs, schools and colleges, workshops, conferences and retreats, treatment centers, youth and elder gatherings—anywhere women want to explore, support one another, and be empowered together.

The activities are mostly secular, but are also appropriate for religious, spiritual, or new age groups (we mean that in a good way). They include psychological activities, creative and exploratory activities, and deeply sacred practices. In some activities you will experience "the sweet territory of silence" and in others you will play and laugh together.

Each activity includes a brief overview, suggested materials, step-by-step guidelines for facilitating the activity, and recommendations for songs, music, books or films related to the activity.

Please visit our website at www.watwabook.com to find a wealth of resources and links to poetry, music, videos, websites and more to support your women's group.

We arranged our activities by seasons, but you can use most at any time. You can mix and match, use them "as is" or modify them. Make these activities your own. On our website, we provide additional discussion questions, more recommendations for music, poetry, books, and videos, and an ever-expanding list of other resources for enriching your groups. The activities can be used with groups of any size or level of experience. Groups can be organized by age, cultural heritage, common interests, profession, or no specific feature other than being women.

Whether your women's group will stay together for a short time or will remain together for years, the activities are designed to help you provide the nutrients, sunshine, water, soil, and stakes in the ground that will help to establish a robust, wild, walled garden of a women's group—a fertile place to meet with women you love, to relax and renew, to plant seeds, watch them grow, harvest the bounty from each season, and be nourished long into the future.

SPRING

1

Doorways

The doors to the world of the wild Self are few but precious. If you have a deep scar, that is a door, if you have an old, old story, that is a door. If you love the sky and the water so much you almost cannot bear it, that is a door. If you yearn for a deeper life, a full life, a sane life, that is a door. ~Clarissa Pinkola Estés

Portals, gates, and doorways are powerful symbols. They can represent the thresholds that lie between the life we have known and the life ahead of us. They symbolize opportunity, hope, new life, initiation, and passages from one world to another. They also pose barriers or limits: the obstacles we must overcome to continue our journey.

Crossing a threshold can signify leaving the known world to enter the sometimes perilous unknown. In mythology, powerful beasts such as lions, dragons, and bulls often guard gates and portals. At times, a riddle must be solved, a password given, or a key found to gain entry. We can be afraid to walk through a doorway even when we can see hints of a better world on the other side.

In this activity, we will identify the doorways, portals, and thresholds we are encountering in our lives at this time, become aware of barriers or opportunities we haven't seen, and discover what actions we might need to take to move forward.

Materials

Personal journals or paper and pen; copied or printed pictures of doorways, gates, portals, and thresholds (one for each member) from books, magazines, or websites

Step-by-Step Guidelines

- Place pictures of doorways, thresholds, and portals face down in the center of the circle.
- Read the activity description on the previous page.
- Ask members to choose one of the facedown images, look at and silently reflect on it.
- After several minutes, ask the following questions, allowing time in between each question for contemplation and journaling:
  o *What would you like to leave behind before you walk through?*
  o *Which of your gifts (strengths) would you like to bring with you?*
  o *What dragon do you fear awaits you if you walk through?*
- Members may share their responses one at a time in the whole group or in dyads or triads. After everyone has answered, you might lead or listen to a guided meditation taking them through the opening, where they will discover something, they've been hoping for on the other side.
- Discussion questions after the meditation can include:
  o *What was it like to step over the threshold?*
  o *What did you find?*
  o *How will that be significant in your life?*

Suggested Resources

Music: Beautiful Chorus - *Pachamama*
            Carrie Newcomer - *The Only Through Is In*
            Norah Jones - *Carry On*

Poetry: Susa Silvermarie - *Her Call to My Wilds*
            Anne Hillman - *We Look with Uncertainty*
            Jelaluddin Rumi - *Don't Go Back to Sleep*

Online: See our website or search for "doorways guided meditation"

2

Meeting Our Future Selves

Look closely at the present you are constructing.
It should look like the future you are dreaming. ~Alice Walker

We are the authors of the future. While we cannot control what happens to us, what other people do, or how the world unfolds over time, we *can* decide how we want to envision and navigate our futures.

Who and how do we want to be? What language do we want to use? What do we want to prioritize, and what do we want to let go of? We can set goals, strategize about how to best reach those goals, and implement our plans. We can dream about the future, worry about it, try to control it, or just go with the flow. And we can use our imagination to connect with a future version of ourselves, one who might hold some important guidance for us, and just might surprise us.

We are invited to time travel in this activity, by imagining a conversation with ourselves 5 years, 10 years, or even 20 years into the future. When we ask our future self questions, the answers she gives can give us clues about how we may want to spend our time in the present. We can imagine that an amazing version of our future self already exists, and she is calling us toward her. As we create a relationship with her over time, she can become one of our guides.

Materials

Personal journals or paper and pens

Step-by-Step Guidelines

- Ask members to decide how many years in the future they want to imagine—5, 10, 20?
- Read and pause between each of these questions for members to write their answers.
  - *What do you enjoy doing almost every day?*
  - *What is your occupation?*
  - *What is your favorite creative outlet?*
  - *What are your family relationships like?*
  - *How do your close friends describe you?*
  - *How do you handle conflicts with other people?*
  - *What kind of home do you live in?*
  - *What is something in your life that _____ years ago you couldn't have imagined?*
  - *What is the most important thing you did to get to where you are today?*
- Allow time for members to share a few of their answers with the group, or in small groups.

Note: An alternative to this "question and written answer" format is to play or read a future self-guided visualization you've found on our website or online and ask members to share their experiences with one another.

Suggested Resources

Music: Brooke Medicine Eagle - *A Gift of Song* (album)
             Des'ree - *You Gotta Be*
Poetry: Amanda Gorman - *The Hill We Climb* and *The Way Forward*
Online: See our website or search for "future self guided visualization"

3

Quick Writes

I write to discover what I know. ~Flannery O'Connor

Expressive writing, or writing briefly about situations in our lives, has proven beneficial for anxiety, depression, post-traumatic stress, college adjustment, relationships, and a variety of physical conditions. A "quick write" is a form of expressive writing consisting of a brief written response to a question or prompt.

While scribbling words in 10-minute quick writes, we often find new meaningful insights we didn't know were buried in our minds and hearts. Our writing may bring light to a situation or a solution our conscious mind has been unable to access. Sometimes what we write makes us laugh or brings us to tears. In an essay in *The New York Times*, Annie Dillard wrote, "At its best, the sensation of writing is that of any unmerited grace." As we become aware of these hidden gems, we can explore them further in our women's group, or with a friend or therapist.

When we write, we might encounter an internal perfectionist—a censor who tells us we must follow all the grammar and punctuation rules, or that we have to be logical, accurate, or clever. Quickly responding to writing prompts can evade the censor, allowing a different voice to emerge, one that is freer and more creative.

Our inner stories and wisdom come forward during this activity, as we respond to one or more writing prompts.

Materials

Personal journals or paper and pens

Step-by-Step Guidelines

- Open the circle by playing music while members gather writing materials and listen quietly.
- Discuss these quick-write instructions from Natalie Goldberg's *Writing Down the Bones*:
  o Keep the hand moving.
  o Don't cross out.
  o Don't worry about spelling, punctuation, or grammar.
  o Lose control.
  o Don't think. Don't get logical.
  o Go for the jugular. If something scary or sad comes up, stay with it.
- Read one of these writing prompts (or one you've chosen) and allow 10 minutes for members to write their responses. You can repeat the exercise with one or more of the other prompts.
  o Write about a time and place where you felt completely cared for.
  o Write about what you would do if you had magical powers for a month.
  o Write about a decision you need to make this year.
  o Write about a difficult situation you are facing.

Suggested Resources

Books: Natalie Goldberg - *Writing Down the Bones: Freeing the Writer Within* (Book and Deck)
Anne Lamott - *Bird by Bird: Some Instructions on Writing and Life*
James W. Pennebaker and Joshua M. Smyth - *Opening Up by Writing It Down: How Expressive Writing Improves Health and Eases Emotional Pain*

Music: Woven Kin - *Down Deeper*
Brandi Carlile and Alicia Keys - *I Have a Voice*

4
Speed "Dating"

Each friend represents a world in us, a world possibly not born until they arrive,
and it is only by this meeting that a new world is born.
~Anais Nin

It's surprising how quickly people can bond when a safe container is created. The spontaneous nature of this ice-breaking exercise doesn't allow members to think through what they want to share ahead of time, which encourages authenticity. This activity is less time-consuming than traditional go-around-the-circle introductions, which can sometimes drag on. It's interesting, often laughter-filled, and can be moving. The questions are just challenging enough for people to feel stretched but not overwhelmed. It's good for introverts who may not feel comfortable sharing in a large group but can be more at ease sharing one-to-one.

Although it is ideal for the first session of a group or when members are just getting to know each other, this activity can also be used with long-standing groups, because it can reveal new things about each member and strengthen relationships between members who already know each other well.

Materials

Loud bell; list of questions/prompts; timer

Step-by-Step Guidelines

- Ask members to stand in two lines facing one another so each woman has a partner, and ask everyone to be quiet. Members can also stand anywhere in the room with a partner. Once women have found a partner, let them know you will be calling out a question or a sentence to complete, and request that they share their answer to each question or prompt with their partner for up to one minute each, and to remain silent after each prompt has been answered.

- Share the first question or prompt and allow two minutes for partners to respond.

- When you ring the bell at the end of two minutes, ask members to thank their partner and silently switch to a new partner. You may need to ring the bell a few times or project your voice to be heard. If members are in lines, ask them to move one step to the left, and the people who end up without a partner to join the end of the other line.

- When the room has quieted, share the second question or prompt, allow sharing for two minutes, ring the bell, and continue until each person has partnered with every other person, or as long as time allows.

- You can use the questions and prompts below or create your own. It is important for the prompts or questions to be a surprise—and that each successive question represents an increasing level of vulnerability or intimacy. Sample prompts:

  o *The main thing that brought me here is . . .*
  o *I live in _____ but I feel most at home in _____ . . .*
  o *Something I want from this group is . . .*
  o *One thing I might do that would get in my way of getting the most out of this group is . . .*
  o *One thing that makes me laugh is . . .*
  o *I am moved to tears by . . .*

Welcoming All That We Are ◆ 43

- *The thing I hold most sacred is . . .*
- *Looking into your eyes reminds me of . . .*
- *Something I commit to bringing to this group is . . .*
- *I may have just met you, but I already love/appreciate you because . . .*

This activity can be used at the beginning of another activity or can be used on its own. When complete, ask members to share how they felt or what they experienced during the activity.

Suggested Resources

Book: Susan Gillis Chapman - *The Five Keys to Mindful Communication: Using Deep Listening and Mindful Speech to Strengthen Relationships, Heal Conflicts, and Accomplish Your Goals*

Music: Kristin Chenoweth - *For Good*
            Jennifer Nettles - *You Will Be Found*

Poetry: Hauntie (May Yang) - *To All My Friends*
            Oriah Mountain Dreamer - *The Invitation*

5

Embracing Self-Care

You are worth the quiet moment. You are worth the deeper breath. You are worth the time it takes to slow down, be still, and rest. ~Morgan Harper Nichols

Often, we can find it easier to be compassionate and supportive with others than to take care of ourselves. Many women find it tough to prioritize self-care. Starting as young girls, overt and implied messages tell us it is selfish to take care of our bodies, our minds, our spirits. Over time, we internalize the belief that putting our own needs on the back burner is the way to please others, to be loved and appreciated, to be a good daughter/mother/wife/partner, or to achieve success at work.

This is a mistaken view. Not only does taking care of our own needs make us healthier, happier, and more resilient, it makes us more available and energized to excel at work, to be fully present at home, and to lift others up. Making self-care part of our daily routine also keeps us from falling into "fake self-care," where we indulge in unhealthy behaviors (spend too much money, drink too much, eat junk food) in the name of "I deserve this."

We need to make time to nourish our spirit and replenish our energy, as well as take care of ourselves physically. Eating nutritious food, getting enough sleep, and moving our bodies are basic needs for all of us, but how we stay energized varies. Introverts require more alone-time activities, while being with others energizes extroverts. Some of us need music, or to be around water, or to be with animals, or time for artistic creativity.

What recharges your batteries? What fills your cup? Take a moment to reflect on the people, places, activities that are renewing or rejuvenating for you. Consider this: if you were someone you loved very much, how would you treat yourself? We review our current personal self-care habits in this activity and commit to making at least one new self-care action part of our routine.

Materials

A large sheet of newsprint or art paper; a bold marker for each woman; a table or cardboard backing

Step-by-Step Guidelines

- Read the activity description and ask women to consider a few ways they are good at taking care of themselves, and a few ways they would like to better take care of themselves.
- Ask members to draw a large circle on their paper and break it into four quadrants. Label one "home and body," one "finance and work," one "emotion and relationship," and one "spirit and soul."
- Ask members to list in each quadrant three ways they *do* take care of themselves well in that domain, and three ways they would like to *expand* their self-care in that domain.
- Ask members to gather in small groups of three to share what they've written, for about five minutes each.
- After this, ask each woman to rest in silence and ask their inner-most self to choose ONE self-care activity they can feasibly add to their lives. Allow it to bubble up without evaluating it. For some it might be "Apply for a new job." For others it might be "Get a monthly pedicure." While some things might feel smaller than others, the *readiness* to do it and *what it means* to do it are the most important things.
- Ask for volunteers to share what they plan to add. Some follow-up discussion questions could be:
  o *Who or what can help you keep your commitment?*
  o *Who or what barrier might get in the way?*

Suggested Resources

Books: Kristin Neff & Christopher Germer - *The Mindful Self-Compassion Workbook: A Proven Way to Accept Yourself, Build Inner Strength, and Thrive*

Alice D. Domar - *Self-Nurture: Learning To Care for Yourself As Effectively As You Care for Everyone Else*

Music: Yola - *Hold On*
          Rhiannon Giddens - *Tomorrow Is My Turn*
          Melody Gardot - *Morning Sun*
Poetry: Barbara Kingsolver - *How To Do Absolutely Nothing*
          Naomi Shihab Nye - *Famous*
          Derek Walcott - *Love After Love*

6
Sacred Bundles

*"That, I think, is the power of ceremony.
It marries the mundane to the sacred.* ~Robin Wall Kimmerer

Cultures throughout the world dating back at least 5,000 years have made sacred bundles, small pouches or wrapped collections of culturally or spiritually meaningful or symbolic objects. Some indigenous and First Nations people of North America refer to these as *medicine bundles* or *medicine bags*. Medicine refers to the spiritual or healing power or blessings imbued into objects. In some traditions, these were carried or worn around the neck throughout one's life—to bring good luck, protection, or strength in battle—and buried with the person. In other Native American Indian traditions, a designated carrier, considered a holy person, held one medicine bundle for the tribe.

In Celtic shamanism, a "crane bag" refers to a small or large bag in which Druids (spiritual leaders, teachers, judges in Ancient Celtic culture) carry shells, rocks, magical objects, feathers, stones, representations of the elements, or ritual tools.

Sacred bundles can be made for protection on a long journey, for healing, to mark a rite of passage, or for navigating everyday life. They can hold items representing important parts of our personal or cultural identity, carved amulets, coins, animal parts, stones, or other memorabilia. A friend, family member, or spiritual guide can give them to us, or we can make them for others.

In this activity, we will make a wrapped collection of symbolic or spiritually significant items meant to guide, heal, protect, or give spiritual support. The bundles can be worn or kept in a special place, perhaps by the bedside or on a personal altar. Over time, items can be added or removed from the bundles, as new challenges and blessings are brought into our lives.

Materials

5-inch squares of cloth or soft leather; twine or heavy thread; crystals, shells, herbs, feathers, beads, coins, bones; other small items each member brings that are spiritually or personally symbolic or meaningful to her

Step-by-Step Guidelines

- Before your meeting, share the activity description with the members, and ask them to bring small items that are personally meaningful, symbolic, or sacred.

- After opening the circle, read the activity description, and show one of the YouTube videos (or send a link to group members in advance), or explain how a sacred bundle is made.

- Ask members to share the meaning of some items in their collection, and what guidance, healing, or wisdom they are seeking. It is also okay for members to keep some or all the items and their meanings private.

- If everyone agrees, members might spend a few moments sending blessings into all the items before assembling their sacred bundles.

- If possible, assemble the bundles outdoors, with each member having their own blanket or table to work on. If indoors, play music or nature sounds while members fill and secure their bundles.

- Allow time for members to share their experiences with the group.

Suggested Resources

Books: don Jose Ruiz - *The Medicine Bag: Shamanic Rituals and Ceremonies for Personal Transformation*

Joanna van der Hoeven - *The Crane Bag: A Druid's Guide to Ritual Tools and Practices*

Music: Curawaka - *Vem Mae Natureza*

Joanne Shenandoah - *Matriarch: Iroquois Women's Songs* (Album)

Putamayo Presents - *Celtic Women* (album)

Online: Search YouTube for "how to make a medicine bag"

7

Our Inner Teacher

. . . people must recognize, first, that they have an inner guidance deep within, and second that they can trust it. ~Shakti Gawain

Each of us has an inner teacher—a guide that can help us make wise decisions and identify our next steps. Different from our thinking mind, the inner teacher is like a wise elder. She often speaks softly and can only be heard when we slow down and become quiet. She sometimes requires that we enter into a non-ordinary state of awareness, through ritual, drumming, creativity, nature, or body movement, to be able to hear what she has to say. She most often uses few words, and delivers only the most essential, boiled down message, such as: *Forgive,* or *Have courage,* or *Say yes,* or *Wait, be patient.*

As women, we have often been taught to ignore our own inner guidance. We have been encouraged to rely on or please external authorities—parents, teachers, ministers—who may have been well-meaning but couldn't know our full experience. Rarely did we receive education on how to use our intuitive knowing to guide our actions, but instead were trained to be rational, to weigh the pros and cons, to ignore our gut feelings.

When we begin to connect with our inner wisdom, we begin to find answers about important decisions, difficult situations, or next steps. We can be guided toward our *own* true north by an inner compass. While we may still need help from others to stay on our path, especially when we get triggered or our lives become chaotic and overwhelming, cultivating an internal GPS (global positioning system) builds our confidence and allows us to live our lives with intention and direction.

This activity encourages us to find the positive characteristics within ourselves that we can access when we want to hear the voice of our inner teacher.

Materials

Personal journals or sketch paper; pens or pencils

Step-by-Step Guidelines

- Ask each circle member to make a list of eight to ten wise people who have positively enhanced her life.

- Ask members to write a word or phrase beside each name that describes the qualities or characteristics they admire about that person.

- Ask each member to close her eyes, dropping into silent awareness for several breaths, and then to locate aspects of herself that embody any of the characteristics that were listed. If a member has trouble locating these aspects of herself, ask her to imagine discovering a new part of herself that possesses these qualities.

- Ask everyone to spend a few minutes writing or sketching the dimensions of themselves that have these qualities. They might consider giving this part of themselves a name, describing what it might look like, or what their voice sounds like.

- Ask members to revisit the list and note the qualities within themselves that mirror those of the people they listed. Ask them to notice which qualities they would like to strengthen.

- Allow time for members to share their inner teacher descriptions or portraits, in dyads or triads for larger groups.

Suggested Resources

Book: Zen Cryar-DeBrucke - *Your Inner GPS: Follow Your Internal Guidance to Optimal Health, Happiness, and Satisfaction*

Music: Lizz Wright - *Singing In My Soul*

        Fearless Soul - *I Am Already Enough*

Poetry: rupi kuar - *home body* and *it was when I stopped searching for home*

8

Drawing Cards

If we would have new knowledge, we must get a whole world
of new questions. ~Suzanne Langer

Throughout the ages, people have used divination tools to help them gain insight, make decisions, or receive guidance. Over 1000 years ago in China, people tossed "I Ching" coins, finding meaning from a book passage corresponding to the pattern of coins. Other cultures have designated an intuitive person or group to provide divine guidance, such as the Oracle of Delphi in Greece.

Some have taken guidance from the way a pendulum swings over map locations or words like "yes" or "no." Often people use symbols on card decks, which later became a system of symbols known as Tarot (based on the Italian word *tarocchi* meaning *of unknown origin*).

A wide variety of oracle cards are available now which are more free form, with less structure than Tarot cards. They are illustrated, often come with a guidebook, and are drawn using intuition. Several decks of oracle or divination cards are available on the Internet and in bookstores, each having a different theme. Whether you believe these practices are random, sometimes result in synchronicities by chance, help people access their own subconscious, or they actually access communications from beyond, many women's groups have found them useful to tap into multiple ways of knowing.

In women's groups, oracle cards can be used as a tool to engage inner wisdom and illuminate fresh perspectives. They can inspire new behaviors that may be helpful during difficult transitions or within relationships or provide guidance for working with unresolved issues.

In this activity, members draw a card from a deck and share the meaning it might have for them. Rather than literal or intellectual meanings, the cards bring information through the power of symbols. Each can have many interpretations, and affect us on mental, emotional, physical, and spiritual levels.

Materials

A deck of oracle or divination cards. Some of our favorites include:

- *Earth Magic Oracle Cards* by Steven Farmer
- *Oracle Card Decks* by Outi Harma at outiart.com
- *Spirits of the Animals Oracle* by Jody Bergsman

Step-by-Step Guidelines

- Open the circle by reading the Joy Harjo poem or one you choose.
- Ask members to close their eyes, breathe deeply, and consider a current unresolved issue in their life, and think of an open-ended question about that issue. For example, *What message do you have for me?* or *How can I be my best self in this situation?*
- Fan the cards and hold them face down. Have each member choose a card from the deck.
- Ask members to focus on the card's image and theme while you play a piece of gentle music or the sound of soft rainfall or a babbling brook.
- Suggest they pay attention to any visions, feelings, or words that arise. Ask each member to share out loud the description on the card or in the guidebook (in triads if the group is larger).
- With a smaller group or more time, you may have women choose two cards, one representing outgoing influences (the past), and one representing incoming influences (into the future). They might also draw one card to represent what they need to address outwardly in their lives and another to represent what they need to attend to within.

Suggested Resources

Music: Drumspyder - *The Mother Rune*

Snatam Kaur - *Earth Prayer*

Poetry: Joy Harjo - *Remember*

9

Meet Your Goddess

Mother Goddess is reawakening, and we can begin to recover
our primal birthright, the sheer, intoxicating joy of being alive. ~Starhawk

For thousands of years, cultures around the world have revered goddesses with powerful attributes like deep wisdom, courage, healing capabilities, divine powers, and even willful destructive energies. Today, the goddess is a symbol of empowerment for women and of the Divine Feminine. The goddess is within all of us. Discovering Kuan Yin (Buddhist goddess of compassion), Artemis (Greek goddess of the hunt), Inanna (Sumerian goddess of love and warfare), Kali (Hindu goddess of destruction), or Brigid (Celtic goddess of fertility) can inspire us to strengthen qualities we haven't fully claimed.

Billie first experienced working with goddesses 30 years ago, during a five-day women's retreat led by Nancee Redmond. Nancee had pasted goddess images on pieces of construction paper and placed them face down on the floor. After a period of silence, each woman chose one of the prepared papers and saw for the first time the goddess she would work with.

The image Billie drew was Oshun, a river deity among the Yorubá people in Nigeria. She was surprised by her choice, and almost embarrassed, because the depiction of Oshun was a rough-hewn, stocky, almost masculine figure standing beside the Oshun River with her arms raised.

To Billie, there was nothing "goddess-like" about the wooden statue. But there was something powerful about the fierce stance of the figure she has found meaningful to this day, especially when she needs to summon strength during difficult times. Also, the symbolism of Oshun standing by her river has been important to Billie throughout the years, because water has been an important symbol for her. Now, when she leads women's groups, using images of goddesses always leads to insightful work.

Materials

Personal journals or paper and pens; copied or printed goddess images from books or the Internet, at least one for each woman in the circle

Step-by-Step Guidelines

- Place the goddess images face down on a table or the floor.
- Play music while each woman chooses an image.
- Allow 20 minutes for each woman to consider and respond in writing to these questions:
  - *What is there about your goddess you like or relate to?*
  - *What do you not like or identify with? Why?*
  - *What is your goddess telling you?*
- Allow time for members to share their answers with the group. In larger circles, break up into dyads or triads so everyone has time to respond to each question.
- Suggest that members display their goddess picture at home and continue to ask her what messages she wants to impart.

Suggested Resources

Books: Jean Shinoda Bolen - *Goddesses in Everywoman: Powerful Archetypes in Women's Lives* and *Goddesses in Older Women: Archetypes in Women Over Fifty*

Music: Women of the Calabash - *Oshun Chant*
Libana - *A Circle is Cast*
Windsong Martin - *Sing to Me Goddess*
Robbie Gass On Wings of Song - *From the Goddess*

Poetry: Audre Lord - *Recreation*

10

Mirrors and Projections I

*We meet ourselves time and time again
in a thousand disguises on the path of life.* ~Carl Jung

In many cultures, mirrors are sewn onto ceremonial costumes or glued to masks, in part to remind us that we are mirrors for each other. Each person we meet, especially those we have strong positive or negative responses to, are mirrors for positive or negative aspects of ourselves we are not aware of or do not want to claim. We tend to project out (kind of like projecting a movie onto the "screen" of another person) what Carl Jung called the *shadow*, aspects of ourselves that we have been unwilling to acknowledge. We then experience these qualities being mirrored back by others.

Angeles Arrien taught that some people in our lives can be a *clear mirror* or a *smoking mirror*. *Clear mirrors* are people we admire or idealize—people that capture our imagination. We may think we cannot be as talented, funny, or skilled as they are, but because we can see these qualities in them, we also have them within ourselves. These potentials within us may not yet have been amplified or developed, but they are there. *Smoking mirrors* are people who we have trouble with. They may irritate us, or they may remind us of difficult people from our past. They may ignite our sense of competitiveness, or critical judgment.

When we respond strongly to someone, we can ask ourselves *Is there any part of this I need to pay attention to within myself?* If your answer is *No way!* you may want to look a little deeper. This activity will help us identify the people in our lives who mirror back to us qualities we may need to attend to or amplify within ourselves.

Materials
Plain, unlined paper; colored pencils, markers

Step-by-Step Guidelines
- Introduce the concepts of mirrors and projections in the activity description.
- Ask members to draw two large boxes on the paper, and label one Clear Mirrors and one Smoking Mirrors.
- Begin playing music and instruct members to draw "frames" around the boxes and fill each box with the names of people in their lives who are their respective mirrors.
- Using the pencils or markers, "decorate" the framed mirrors using colors that represent how they feel about the people they chose as mirrors.
- Allow time for members to share their drawings and ask them to bring the drawings to your next meeting. They will be used in the following activity.

Suggested Resources
Book: Angeles Arrien - *The Four-Fold Way: Walking the Paths of the Warrior, Teacher, Healer, and Visionary* (the Way of the Visionary chapter)

Music: The Wailin' Jennys - *One Voice*
Loreena McKinnitt - *The Mask and Mirror* (album)
Poetry: Nikki Giovanni - *You Came, Too*

11
Mirrors and Projections II

The way we experience the world around us
is a direct reflection of the world within us. ~Gabrielle Bernstein

The previous activity introduced the concepts of *clear mirrors, smoking mirrors,* and *projections,* and helped identify the people who are our metaphorical mirrors. These are people we encounter who can help us integrate the unclaimed positive and negative aspects of ourselves—helping us to become more whole and complete. To expand on this notion, Angeles Arrien described *five stages of projection:*

1. We find a person to hold our projection. If we do not see ourselves as leaders or as attractive, we idealize people with those qualities. We may put them on a pedestal, not seeing them as they are but as we want them to be. On the other hand, we may encounter someone who really gets under our skin. We dislike them, and just can't seem to shake it off.

2. The projection begins to fade. We begin to see ways the person does not fit the black and white view we hold of them. We may start to notice flaws in the person we idealized but will rationalize their behavior to maintain the projection and the relationship. We may notice ways that the person who annoyed us has positive traits too but will tend to ignore or minimize those.

3. The projection totally falls off. If we idealize someone, we become disappointed and judgmental about the person. Now we can choose to either move to stage four or find another person to idealize. Many people repeat these three stages over and over, discarding relationships along the way.

4. We recognize that a lot of the issues we had around this person were our own stuff. We see our part in creating a story about the other person that was not true.

5. We integrate the projection, claiming our positive qualities, and acknowledging and working on our challenges. We may end up having a healthy relationship with the person, or we may need to distance from or leave the relationship when we realize the overlay, we've been putting on them isn't real.

This activity reveals more about how we project our positive or negative unclaimed qualities onto others.

Materials

The previous activity's *mirror* drawings; a copy of the activity description for each member

Step-by-Step Guidelines

- Before your next meeting make copies of the activity description and remind members to bring their *mirror* drawings from the previous meeting.
- At the meeting, ask members to refer to their drawings where they identified *clear mirrors* and *smoking mirrors*, and add more names if they would like to.
- Distribute the handout and ask members to maintain silence while they read and consider the information as it relates to the people they identified.
- Ask that they reflect upon their relationship with at least *one person from each mirror* with whom they have or had an important relationship, in light of the five stages of projection.
- Allow time for each member to share her reflections, or about other projections she is aware of after completing this process.

Suggested Resources

Books: Angeles Arrien - *The Four-Fold Way: Walking the Paths of the Warrior, Teacher, Healer, and Visionary*
Robert Johnson - *Understanding Psychological Projection*

Music: Nicola Cruz - *Folha de Jurema*
Fleetwood Mac - *Landslide*
Loreena McKinnitt - *The Book of Secrets* (album)

12
Priority Pie

When you recover or discover something that nourishes your soul and brings joy, care enough about yourself to make room for it in your life.
~Jean Shinoda Bolen

What are our core priorities? What is most important to us? What are the essential components of our primary purpose, our reason for being? And is how we spend our time, attention, and energy in alignment with our main goals?

Examples of priorities might be health, family, helping people, creating art, social justice, being present for an aging parent, living our spiritual principles or religious values, recovery or personal growth, professional development, furthering our education, caring for our children, and many more.

We clarify our personal priorities in this activity, so we can be sure to make space for them in our lives. It is a good exercise to repeat every year, to see if our priorities have shifted, and how we might rebalance our lives to support our new goals.

Materials

Personal journals or paper and pens; blank papers with a large circle with a dot in the center for creating "pie charts" (You can create or download and print from the Internet.); pens, pencils, crayons, markers

Step-by-Step Guidelines

- After opening the circle, read the activity description, and ask members to write a list of their priorities.

- Ask members to share their lists with one another, encouraging them to change, add, or remove items from their lists as they are inspired by other members and gain clarity.

- Have members make a pie chart that shows their true priorities—what they currently hold most sacred and think of as most important in their lives. For example, a slice of the pie might be family, another might be work or school, one slice might be travel or a hobby, another might be exercise or nutrition, and another might be work on issues of concern to them such as social justice, equity, environmental sustainability, etc.

- Next, ask members to make a new pie chart that shows how they spend their time, energy, and resources now. Outside of sleep, ask women to estimate the proportion of time they spend on the main activities of their lives—work, exercise, parenting, volunteering, commuting, cooking/cleaning, leisure time, TV/social media.

- Lead a discussion based on these questions:
  o *What do you notice when you compare your two pie charts? Is the way you spend your time in alignment with your priorities?*
  o *Is there anything you'd like to let go of, add, reduce, or increase in either chart?*
  o *What kind of support do you need?*

- Allow time for each woman to answer this important question:
  o *What is the first action you will take to align your time with your priorities?*

Suggested Resources

Books: Jennifer Loudon - *The Life Organizer: A Woman's Guide to a Mindful Year*

Mary Oliver - *Upstream: Selected Essays*

Music: Grace Potter and the Nocturnals - *Things I Never Needed*

Miley Cyrus - *The Climb*

Sia - *Courage to Change*

13

Summer Solstice

I am summer, come to lure you away from your computer...
come dance on my fresh grass, dig your toes into my beaches.
~Oriana Green

Summer Solstice, in the third week of June, is the longest day of the year in the Northern Hemisphere. Throughout history, people around the world have celebrated it with nature festivals, dancing, and bonfires to guarantee a good harvest for the fall. Many Native Americans still practice solstice rituals, and thousands of people congregate at Stonehenge in England each year to celebrate the Summer Solstice. Though not directly related to the solstice, midsummer also celebrates Juneteenth, a good time to join our Black sisters in commemorating the end of slavery in the United States in the 1860s.

Summer is the season when all the promises of autumn, winter, and spring are fulfilled. Our faith in the generative nature of Mother Earth is restored. Her energy and abundance invite us to celebrate and delight in nature. Our gardens are full of juicy fruits and nourishing vegetables. Although a few weeds may appear, our communities of women are grateful to be able to tend our summer gardens together, enjoy the energy of the sun, and appreciate refreshing waters.

This activity invites our women's groups to gather, share music and poetry, and weave wreaths from herbs and flowers to wear as we celebrate together.

Materials

Fresh and artificial vines, garlands, herbs, flowers; strong raffia or wire; ribbons; sparkling beverages

Step-by-Step Guidelines

- Before your meeting, ask members to bring fresh flowers or greenery from their gardens.
- At the meeting, ask members to add the flowers and greenery to the "altar" or center.
- Share music, poems, and the activity description.
- Ask members to reflect on these questions:
  - *What new or favorite activity are you enjoying this summer?*
  - *What weeds are among the flowers in your garden?*
  - *What is one of your favorite memories of summer?*
- While considering their responses to the questions, members create crown-like wreaths using natural materials and ribbons woven into raffia or wire.
- Repeat the questions and allow time for members to share their responses.
- Ask members to secure their crowns on their heads.
- Celebrate together with traditional music, circle dancing, and sparkling beverages.

Suggested Resources

Music: Michael Franti - *Sound of Sunshine*
        Iris Stewart - *Sacred Woman, Sacred Dance*
        Elaine Silver - *By the Earth*
        Meghan Trainer - *Better When I'm Dancin'*
Poetry: Mary Oliver - *The Summer Day*
Online: Search YouTube for "summer solstice music"

SUMMER

14

Gratitude Bullet Journal

Wear gratitude like a cloak and it will feed every corner of your life.
~Jelaluddin Rumi

Wisdom traditions and science both tell us the practice of expressing gratitude is healthy for our mind, body, and spirit. If we can notice and appreciate the simple gifts in each day, we can find more peace and joy in the here and now. Even in difficult periods of our lives, attending to what we are grateful for can be an antidote to stress— whether it is access to fresh food or hot running water, special people in our lives, pets we love, or aspects of our home or environment.

When we look for the positives and note them in a gratitude journal, we teach our brains that the good deserves just as much attention as the not-so-good. Over time a more positive mindset is formed, and we become more resilient. When we truly lose hope during a particularly dark time, we can review our gratitude journal to remind us of the blessings we've received.

A bullet journal is a method of journaling that uses color coding, icons, charts, and bullet lists to track various aspects of our lives, from schedules to progress toward goals. A gratitude bullet journal uses these, along with art, sketches, pictures, or symbols, to make our practice of gratitude multilayered and fun.

It is helpful to have tools for establishing new practices. In this activity, we create a tool for practicing gratitude that members can continue to use at home.

Materials

Blank journal, or booklets of stapled together paper (lined, grid pages or dotted pages are great, but not necessary); a table or hard backing for writing/drawing; fine tip pens, colored pencils; rulers, stickers, Washi tape

Step-by-Step Guidelines

- Before you meet, ask members to bring a blank journal and art supplies they would like to use. Provide several pages of stapled-together paper to members without journals. Suggest they search Google, Pinterest, and Instagram for bullet journal ideas.

- Ask members to arrange their supplies and assure everyone there is no right way to create the journals; each one will be different.

- Take quiet time or play music while members decorate the cover and beginning pages.

- Unless their journals already have lines or grids, members will begin by dividing one or more pages into daily blocks for a month or more into the future.

- In each block, provide space for noting what members are grateful for. This could be titled *Grateful for . . .* and consist of blank lines to fill in, a spot for sketching something each day, or another way to document their gratitude daily.

- Suggest members begin by filling in today's section—expressing their gratitude for a few things and sharing that with the group.

- Discuss how people feel about committing to a daily gratitude practice. Some useful questions:
  - *What time of day and where would you like to do this gratitude practice?*
  - *What conditions can you put into place to make it more likely?*
  - *What might keep you from following through with this commitment?*

Suggested Resources

Books: Ryder Carroll - *The Bullet Journal Method: Track the Past, Order the Present, Design the Future*

Anne Lamott - *Help, Thanks, Wow: The Three Essential Prayers*

Music: Rita Wilson - *Grateful*

Beautiful Chorus - *Thank You for Your Blessings*

Benadetta Caretta - *You Raise Me Up*

Ann Reed - *My Grateful Heart*

Natalie Merchant - *Kind and Generous*

Poetry: Ellen Bass - *The Sound of Their Names*

Jelaluddin Rumi - *The Guest House*

Online: Search Google Images, Pinterest, or Instagram for examples of bullet journals

15
Labyrinth Journey

The labyrinth is a spiritual tool meant to awaken us to the deep rhythm that unites us to ourselves and to the light that calls from within.
~Lauren Artress

A labyrinth is a type of maze that has only one pathway in and out. For thousands of years, people have used labyrinths as a metaphorical journey through the twists and turns of life, a meditative path to self-discovery or healing, and a place to pray or ask for guidance with a decision or a problem.

Walking the labyrinth has become known throughout the western world primarily through the leadership and writings of Lauren Artress, who has helped to establish permanent labyrinths across the United States. She founded Veriditas, an organization that centers around the Labyrinth Experience as a practice for personal growth and community building.

How the labyrinth "works" is a mystery, but on the scores of walks Billie has taken, answers to the questions she asked have always come, even when her question was simply *What is here for me to learn today?* That question provides good practice in letting go of predetermined expectations and staying open to whatever comes.

A labyrinth walk has three main parts: walking toward the center, pausing in the center, and walking back out. You may be "in the question" as you walk in and connected to spiritual beliefs as you approach the labyrinth's center, which represents oneness or wholeness. The walk out can be a time to integrate any insights that may have come. This activity takes us to a place where we can quiet our mind and hear our own wisdom.

Materials

Personal journals or paper and pens; a local labyrinth or finger labyrinth. It's likely there is a labyrinth somewhere in your area, but if not, you can print downloadable finger labyrinths for members to "walk" at your meeting.

Step-by-Step Guidelines

- Arrange for members to meet at a labyrinth to walk it together.
- Share the activity description with the group.
- Share with the group that although there is no one right way to use a labyrinth, some suggestions may make the walk a more meaningful experience:
  - Before entering the labyrinth, pause in silence. Begin listening for or reflecting on what you want from your walk. It could be the answer to a question, a healing, the resolution of a problem, forgiveness, divine grace, or simply a quiet meditative stroll.
  - Ask your spiritual guide to be present during your walk by invoking a prayer, a hymn, a blessing, or a favorite poem.
  - Remind everyone if they walk the path in and get to the center and clarity isn't there, they will have another chance on the path out.
  - Begin walking toward the center at your pace, following the path. You may think of this as walking toward your own center where you connect with your heart or your divine spirit.
  - When you reach the center, pause. You may want to sit or lie down, give thanks, listen more deeply, sing, dance, or meditate.
  - Begin to walk outward. Stay conscious of your intention for the walk. This is when some people receive a gift of clarity or a sense of well-being and oneness.
  - If you have not received what you wanted, do not be discouraged. Often the conscious mind does not know immediately what you learned; the answer may come later.
  - Before leaving the labyrinth, pause and give thanks.

- Examples of open-ended questions for members to ask:
  - *What is the next best thing for me to do about my health concerns?*
  - *How can I improve my relationship with my family members?*
  - *What do I need to know to improve my work situation?*
  - *Where do I need forgiveness or to forgive?*
- Allow time for members to journal and share their experience with the group.

Suggested Resources
Book: Lauren Artress - *Walking a Sacred Path: Rediscovering the Labyrinth as a Spiritual Tool*
Music: Gabrielle Roth - *Labyrinth*
        Crystal Bowersox - *Up to the Mountain*
Online: Search for "labyrinth locator" or "finger labyrinth"

16

Exploring Creativity

The absolute requirement for creativity is blindfolding the Judge.
~Joan Borysenko

The essence of creativity is using your imagination. You can move beyond traditional ideas, rules, and patterns, and find ways to express some part of your individual or our collective human experience. In our women's groups, we can redefine creativity, and offer each other support to feel safe. While being creative, we can enter into flow states that feel timeless and effortless—like something is coming through us rather than us "manufacturing" something.

Many of us wish we were more creative or talented but believe we did not inherit the "creative gene." Perhaps a family member said we couldn't sing in tune or dance well, and we carried those critiques into adulthood. Maybe a teacher told us our artistic efforts were all wrong. Maybe we put our creativity aside to support others' hopes and dreams. Or, you may be an artist, but have lost some of the spontaneity, playfulness, and joy that comes with creating without a goal.

One key to unlocking our creative gifts is to recall the activities we enjoyed when we were children, like playing with clay, fabrics, or cooking ingredients. We pretended to be great chefs, teachers, doctors, or famous rock stars.

Making collages in small groups instead of individually can be a way to reduce the anxiety of doing something "artistic." It can silence our self-critic or the internalized judgmental voices that keep us from enjoying creative exploration. Our collages don't need to please anyone, earn us money, or inspire others—we can create them just for fun. This activity lets us express some of the things we do not have words for and emphasizes the process rather than the product.

Materials

Sturdy poster boards or butcher paper; magazines for cutting out pictures; glue sticks; colored pencils, markers

Step-by-Step Guidelines

- Before your next circle gathering, ask members to bring several images they think are beautiful, or anything that represents creativity to them—pictures of favorite paintings or women of all ages and ethnicities, pages of sheet music, or nature scenes.
- Lead a short discussion around the following questions:
  o *How do you define creativity?*
  o *When you were young, what were you told about your artistic ability?*
  o *Who encouraged creative play in your home?*
- Distribute the above materials and break into small groups of three or four to work together creating collages that represent their feelings about women's creativity.
- Lead another discussion about the process. Questions might be:
  o *Were there any obstacles to you enjoying this activity, like perfectionism or the voice of your self-critic?*
  o *What is your personal form of creativity?*
  o *What other form of creativity are you called on to explore?*
  o *How could you include more creative activities in your life?*
- Allow time for each group to share their collage.

Suggested Resources

Books: Julia Cameron - *The Artist's Way: 25th Anniversary Edition*
　　　Elizabeth Gilbert - *Big Magic: Creative Living Beyond Fear*
Music: Corinne Bailey Rae - *Put Your Records On*
　　　Carrie Newcomer - *I Will Sing a New Song*
Poetry: Julia Myers - *A Poem*
　　　Annie Lighthart - *The Second Music*
　　　Anais Nin - *Risk*

17

Who Am I?

You know . . . no matter what you do, people are going to expect you to be someone you're not. But if you're clever and lucky and work your butt off, then you get to be surrounded by people who expect you to be the person you wish you were
~Charlie Jane Anders

How do we define who we are as women, and as people? For some of us, the pressure to conform to others' expectations, especially in this age of constant exposure to social media, has left us wondering who we should be.

Hearing other group members' self-definitions and having them bear witness to our own can help expand our sense of self, and often reveals characteristics we aren't aware of. When we learn more about ourselves, we can develop a clearer sense of identity that can help us steer our lives toward more meaningful and fulfilling experiences. The more we know about who we truly are, the easier it becomes to make choices that align with *our* affinities, hopes, dreams, values, and priorities (rather than those we've been told we should have).

Our lives are more joyful when we can just be ourselves, when we stand on the solid ground of our own core beliefs. This simple activity allows us to inquire about the many ways we define ourselves, and perhaps discover aspects of ourselves we hadn't considered before. It relies a bit on the element of surprise, and the spontaneous nature of the responses to the prompts.

Materials

Personal journals or paper and pens

Step-by-Step Guidelines

- Ask members to get into dyads, facing one another.
- One member of the dyad will ask her partner *Who are you?* 20 times, and her partner will quickly write her answers down. Each answer will begin with *I am . . . .* The asker keeps track of the number of responses and says *Thank you* to each response, followed by the same question, *Who are you?*
- Ask each partner to share what it was like to be the asker and the respondent. Then the partners should switch roles and repeat the exercise.
- Returning to the full circle, ask the women to share their insights.
- Questions might include:
  - *Were you surprised by anything you wrote?*
  - *Did you define yourself mostly by roles, qualities, or in other ways?*
  - *Are there any roles, characteristics, or identities on your list you would like to let go of?*
  - *What are some new ways of defining yourself you would like to explore?*

Suggested Resources

Music: Ricki Byers Beckwith - *In the Land of I Am*
   Chaka Khan - *I'm Every Woman*
   Holly Near - *You Can Know All I Am*
   John Astin - *Love, Serve, Remember*
Poetry: Joy Harjo - *Eagle Poem*
   Mark Nepo - *Crossing Some Ocean in Myself*

18

Asking for Help

May you use those gifts that you have received, and pass on the love that has been given to you . . . ~Saint Teresa of Avila

We are not alone when we hesitate to ask for help because we don't want to feel needy or weak. We don't like to impose on friends, or let people know that we don't have it all together. The reality is most people *like* to help. They feel honored that we've trusted them in a time of need.

Sometimes we can experience the opposite—wondering why people are *not* offering help when it seems obvious, we need it. We feel like we shouldn't have to ask, or if we do have to ask, it somehow diminishes the value of the help that is offered. Interestingly, many people (like the wonderful men in our lives) truly have no idea what we need or want until we ask. For some, offering help can seem intrusive, or condescending. Their attitude is *She knows I'm here, if she needs help, she will ask for it.* This makes it important for us to learn how to skillfully ask for help.

We are emotionally stronger when we find a balance between independence and dependence, and that takes practice. This activity explores our beliefs about asking for help.

Materials

Personal journals or blank paper; a copy of the following two pairs of questions for each member:

What did you need help with, and from whom?
How did you feel about not getting the help?
     and
What did you need help with, and from whom?
How did you feel when you received the help?

Step-by-Step Guidelines

- Hand out the above discussion questions face down. Ask members to write for 10 minutes about a time when they asked for help and *didn't* receive it.
- Break into dyads and have partners share their responses to questions (1) and (2) above.
- Next, ask members to write for 10 minutes about a time when they asked for help and *did* receive it.
- Ask members to find a new partner and share their responses to questions (3) and (4) above.
- When the circle comes back together, lead a discussion around these questions:
    - *What were the messages you got growing up about asking for help?*
    - *How does it feel when someone else asks you for help?*

Suggested Resources

Book: Brené Brown - *Daring Greatly*
Music: Sara Bareilles - *A Safe Place To Land*
        Nora Jones - *Help Me Make It Through the Night*
        Sia - *I'm in Here*
Poetry: Hafiz - *Dropping Keys (feminine version)*
        Lisel Mueller - *When I Am Asked*

19

Letting Go

In those moments when we realize how much we cannot control,
we can learn to let go. ~Sharon Salzberg

This activity gives us a tool for letting go of worry and anxiety about our lives, or about a difficult situation for which we haven't found a solution. These can be worries about our health, our family, an event in the future, or some negative trait we want to let go of, like impatience or perfectionism. We will create a small box with a slit in the lid or a top that opens, write what is worrying us on slips of paper, and tuck them into the box. We might call it a *Surrender Box,* a *God Box,* or anything that taps into our spiritual belief system—*Spirit Box, Goddess Box,* or *Angel Box*—whatever is meaningful for us.

The intention is to let these worries go or turn them over to something greater than us. Embellishing the boxes makes them special and is fun to do with other women. After decorating them, we write down a few problems we are struggling with and place them in the box. Once we take the box home, we can continue to add new worries to it when we want to surrender them to a higher power.

When one of the concerns comes to mind again, we can tell ourselves *Rest easy. That is out of my hands,* and be less tempted to keep revisiting it. This can help us be less anxious and more open to recognizing solutions that present themselves. When we truly let go of a problem, and stop controlling, fixing, worrying, or interfering, often we discover it resolves itself in ways we couldn't have imagined.

Materials
Small boxes; art papers; washi tape; markers; beads, stickers

Step-by-Step Guidelines
- Before your next meeting ask members to bring a small box or other container and art materials to share.
- Read the activity description.
- Allow about 30 minutes for members to decorate their boxes, and another 10 minutes for writing their worries on slips of paper.
- Ask members to share what they are going to call their box and invite them to share the worries they are letting go of (if they wish), as they tuck the papers into their boxes. This can be done in dyads or triads for larger groups.
- After the sharing, celebrate releasing worries and anxiety by high-fiving, holding hands in a circle, or dancing together to some upbeat music.

Suggested Resources
Music: Celtic Woman - *Walk Beside Me*
        Frozen Soundtrack - *Let It Go*
        Carol Woods - *Let It Be*
Poetry: Safire Rose - *She Let Go*
        Joy Harjo - *Prepare*

20

Basket Poetry

Show up, show up, show up, and after a while
the muse shows up, too. ~Isabel Allende

Whether we have ever written a poem or not, this activity is a fun way to awaken the inner poet who resides in every woman's imagination. Yep, all of us! With poetry we can express truths about life, about nature, or about ourselves, that cannot be expressed in any other way.

Poems don't need to rhyme, and they don't need to make sense. They can express the most profound aspects of our experience, or the simplest. Serious or silly, gentle, or fierce, short or long, it's completely up to us.

Rather than being faced with a blank sheet of paper, this activity uses words we draw at random to give us a head start. Kind of like training wheels, the words we choose can provide a framework for our expression to thrive. We often find that the words we draw end up being exactly the words that we need to work with. Other times, they encourage us to stretch, to be brave, to be absurd, to play!

We are often surprised at the meaningful poems that result from playing with words in this way. It is likely the inner critic will show up, but there are *no rules* in this poem-making experience! It is fine to change the words from nouns to verbs, singular to plural, add conjunctions, trade words with other members, or choose more words from the basket.

Materials

Personal journals or paper and pens; a basket full of cut-up words printed on heavy paper. See our website for a full page of words to cut up. Add more words if you would like to, and you can make copies based on the size of your group—15-20 words per member is good.

Step-by-Step Guidelines

Read the activity description and the excerpts below to give members a sense of how infinitely varied poetry can be.

. . . I didn't want any flowers, I only wanted
To lie with my hands turned up and be utterly empty.
How free it is, you have no idea how free—
The peacefulness is so big it dazes you . . .
~Excerpt, Sylvia Plath's *Tulips*

. . . Every leaf speaks to me
Fluttering from the Autumn tree . . .
~Excerpt, Emily Bronte's *Fall, Leaves, Fall*

Eagle born of night
Trees swish my hair
Clock ticks, heart beats, moon sets
I rest.
~Anonymous

- Pass the basket of words around; each member will take a handful of words and use them to create a poem.

- Members can choose to use only the words from the basket or can sprinkle them throughout the poem they write.

- Encourage everyone to play with form as well as meaning. Mention that poems won't be critiqued.

- Maintain silence for 20-30 minutes for poem making. Remind women halfway through that if their inner critic pops up, they can gently tell her that her voice is not needed.

- Allow time for members to share their poems. Remind people listening that they are meant to witness other members with curiosity and compassion and listen closely, not only to the words but also to the spaces between the words.

Suggested Resources

Poetry: Anonymous - *The Pen*

Online: Search for short snippets of poetry

21

Mindful Decision Making

Don't try to comprehend it with your mind. Your mind is very limited.
Use your intuition. ~Madeleine L'Engle

It can be hard to make small decisions, like what to eat or whether to accept a social invitation, much less big decisions like whether to take a job or leave a relationship. When we rely only on our minds to make decisions, we leave out important information that our body, emotions, and spirit hold for us. When making decisions, sometimes we get stuck in black or white "either/or" thinking. This can lead to deer-in-the-head-lights decision paralysis—an internal stalemate arising from conflicting needs, desires, and responsibilities.

Cognitive science teaches us that we often make decisions based on assumptions we are not even aware of, and built-in rules that can lead to choices that are not in alignment with our values and goals. In other words, we don't always know why we make the decisions we do. A host of biases that we are not conscious of can lead us into making decisions that baffle our friends, and us, when we look back. Examples are the "sunk cost" bias, where we continue with a situation that is not working because we've already invested so much into it, or the "ostrich effect," when we ignore negative things that seem obvious to others.

When we consult aspects of ourselves beyond our thinking mind, we can make wiser decisions. In this activity, women are introduced to a method for making decisions that draws upon the wisdom of not only the mind, but also the body, the heart or emotions, the gut or intuition, and a deeper source (God, Goddess, Source, Spirit Guides, Higher Self, Awareness).

This can be a large decision, like whether to take a job offer, or a small one, like what to have for dinner. The purpose of the exercise is not necessarily to make a huge decision. It is to learn a *process* for decision-making.

Materials

Personal journals or paper and pens

Step-by-Step Guidelines

- Read the activity description and ask members to reflect on a situation about which they need to make a decision.

- Now, ask members to write down what their **minds** are telling them about the decision. You might tell members, *You will know it's your thinking mind because it is often opinionated, and can be like a Ping-Pong game, or a jury with many voices weighing in. Write down a few of the key pros and cons.*

- Next, ask members to close their eyes and connect with their **hearts,** or their emotional selves. You could ask members, *What does your feeling self say? Usually this is one or two simple sentences, not paragraphs. Write these down.*

- Third, ask members to bring their attention to their abdomen, and reveal what their **gut instinct** says about the situation. You could say, *This is often a very simple word or a few words, like "Go" or "Stay" or "Wait" or "Take the job."*

- Finally, ask members to release all these thoughts and feelings, and sense what their **highest self**, the God or Goddess within, or their deepest wisdom says. At times, this might not even be words, but just a felt sense. If they have trouble connecting, ask them to imagine what a guardian angel or future self might say.

- Allow time for members to write or draw what came to them, then share with the group or in a dyad or triad what they learned from the process.

Suggested Resources

Books: Pema Chodron - *The Places That Scare You: A Guide to Fearlessness in Difficult Times*
Joan Halifax - *Standing at the Edge: Finding Freedom Where Fear and Courage Meet*
Music: Carrie Newcomer - *Learning To Sit Without Knowing*
Poetry: Mary Oliver - *Mornings at Blackwater*

22

Reading the Runes

The Rune means to me that I must strive to live the ordinary life in a non ordinary way. This is what it says in The Book of Runes. Take heart, in the spirit you are always beginning. ~Denny Taylor

The word *rune* comes from the Old English *run*, meaning *mystery*, or *whispered secret*. Beginning in the first century CE, people are thought to have consulted runes, small tiles engraved with letters from an ancient Norse/Germanic language, for guidance or to gain insight about a problem. Each symbol is thought to represent a concept, such as "torch" or "wealth" or "journey." In addition to being symbolic, the letters themselves are thought to hold power, and were sometimes carved on swords.

Today, rune sets are often made of wood, stone, or ceramic, and usually come with a pouch and guidebook that explains what each rune is and what it represents. There are many forms of "casting" or reading the runes.

A simple way to use them is to pose an open-ended question, draw one rune from the pouch, read the meaning, and reflect on how it applies to you. Or, you might draw three runes to represent the past, present, and future. In this activity, members are asked to reflect on an issue they are facing, draw a rune, and share how it might be related to their situation.

Materials

One or more sets of runes (found online, in bookstores, and in "new age" shops)

Step-by-Step Guidelines

- Ask members to breathe deeply, bring their attention to the present moment, and observe several minutes of silence.
- Taking turns, ask members to focus on an issue or a situation about which they need more insight or information. For example, *The issue is my career,* or *What do I need to know about my relationship?* If no specific issue comes to mind, they can ask an open-ended question, like *What do I need to pay attention to in my life now?* They may share the question aloud if they choose.
- One at a time, members will reach into the pouch and draw a rune.
- The member may read aloud the rune's interpretation in the guidebook or ask another member to read the interpretation.
- In a large women's circle, it is best to break up into dyads or triads. In small groups, members can take turns sharing the meaning of the rune or their response to it.
- Ask each member to sketch the rune she drew on a piece of paper and carry it with her in the coming week.

Suggested Resources

Music: Munknörr - *Futharuna*
        Chakra's Dream - *Mystery of the Runes*
Online: Search for "rune meanings and how to use them"

23

Loving Our Bodies

*Being a healthy woman isn't about getting on a scale or measuring your waistline.
We need to start focusing on what matters—on how we feel,
and how we feel about ourselves.* ~Michelle Obama

How many of us would answer *Great!* if asked how we feel about our body? Because we are constantly inundated with unrealistic and unattainable images on television, billboards, and social media that indicate a specific body type (slender and sexy) is the only acceptable one, it's not surprising that we don't always feel okay about our bodies. The first diet book was written in 1860, and today the billion-dollar diet industry continues to sell us the idea that we aren't good enough.

It's doubtful we go through even one day without hearing another woman say something derogatory about her body, and often our own self-critic chimes in. No matter what size or shape our bodies are, we deserve love and respect, especially from ourselves! Instead, we focus a lot of energy on losing weight, comparing ourselves to others, and berating ourselves, and less energy on appreciating *what our bodies can do* and on *how to become more mentally and physically healthy*, no matter our BMI, weight, or size.

Luckily, there is a body positivity movement afoot that can help us overcome our misconceptions about what is beautiful, and even what is healthy. Research shows that when we first improve our body image, we can move on to improving our overall health. This activity encourages us to be more accepting and loving towards our bodies, which paradoxically leads to being mentally and physically healthier.

Materials

Personal journals or paper and pens

Step-by-Step Guidelines

- Ask members to stand and move/stretch/dance to one music selection and/or read a poem. See Suggested Resources below.
- Read the information in the activity description and ask members to write their responses to the following questions or statements. Ask members to share their responses to each question or statement. with the circle.
  - *What are three things you appreciate about your appearance? For example:* **My eyes are a pretty color.**
  - *Write one affirmation about your body you can say every day. For example:* **My body deserves love.**
  - *List three ways your body helps you enjoy life. For example:* **I enjoy swimming.**
  - *What is one unhelpful or unrealistic assumption you could dispute now? For example:* **I can't be happy until I change my appearance.**
  - *What is one goal you have to improve your health that doesn't involve weight? For example:* **I want to try a yoga class.**
- Allow time for members to share their thoughts.
- Close the circle with a poem and moving/stretching/dancing to another piece of music.

Suggested Resources

Books: Sonja Renee Taylor - *The Body Is Not an Apology, Second Edition: The Power of Radical Self-Love* and *Your Body Is Not an Apology Workbook: Tools for Living Radical Self-Love*

Jessamyn Stanley - *Every Body Yoga: Let Go of Fear, Get on the Mat, Love Your Body*

Music: Christina Aguilera - *Beautiful*

Poetry: Kate Baer - *Nothing Tastes as Good as Skinny Feels*

Lucille Clifton - *homage to my hips* and *what the mirror said*

Barbara Kingsolver - *How To Lose That Stubborn Weight*

24

Five Questions

A question is a powerful thing, a mighty use of words.
~Krista Tippett

A sking compelling questions is one of the best ways to pay meaning-ful attention to and learn more about the people in our lives. The same is true when we ask questions of ourselves. When we become detectives of our own experience, we are sometimes surprised by what is revealed. Questions cultivate an open mind and lead us to new knowledge. Asking what touches our hearts or inspires us can reveal our values and help us rediscover what brings joy into our lives. We learn more about what is important to us, and what holds deeper meaning.

Self-inquiry can facilitate greater understanding and even a break-through when dealing with a difficult situation. Carl Jung said *The right question is already half the solution to a problem*. It often leads to self-discov-ery—that *aha* moment when new insights suddenly become clear, and we can move forward into problem-solving.

An exercise by Angeles Arrien inspired this activity, which focuses on one core practice—asking evocative questions that encourage self-reflection.

Materials

Personal journals or paper and pens

Step-by-Step Guidelines

- Ask members to answer the following questions in writing, one at a time. Suggest that members not overthink their answers. Often the first one that comes to mind is asking to be attended to or provides valuable information.
  - *What surprised me today (or this week, this month, this year)?*
  - *What moved me or touched my heart today (or this week, this month, this year)?*
  - *What inspired me today? (or this week, this month, this year)?*
  - *What is weighing on my heart today? (or this week, this month, this year)?*
  - *What do I need to do to move forward today? (or this week, this month, this year)?*
- Ask members to share all their written answers with one another in dyads or small groups.
- An alternative is to first divide members into dyads or small groups, ask the questions one at a time, and members answer the questions verbally within their group.

This activity can serve as an end-of-day journaling exercise to deepen the experience of daily life. The group might agree to do this for a week or more and share their experiences with this practice at the next meeting.

Suggested Resources

Book: Angeles Arrien - *The Fourfold Way: Walking the Paths of the Warrior, Teacher, Healer, and Visionary*

Music: Indigo Girls - *Closer to Fine*
             Katie Melua - *Fields of Gold*

Poetry: Alice Walker - *Reassurance*

25

Creating Mandalas

Making a mandala is a universal activity,
a self-integrating ritual. ~Pema Chodron

M*andala* in Sanskrit means sacred circle. It is derived from the word *mandra,* which means "container of essence." Natural mandalas are found throughout nature, from the rings of an ancient redwood tree to spider webs, seashells, and more. Creating a mandala (a circular image, typically with a central focal point and colorful, detailed, and symbolic designs) has been a contemplative practice across cultures for millennia.

The founder of Depth Psychology, Carl Jung, believed that working with mandalas helps us integrate the various threads of ourselves and leads to feelings of wholeness. Viewing or making mandalas is an active meditation that encourages us to stay in the present moment. Like labyrinth walking, mandala work can allow us to gain insight into decisions, without thinking directly about the problem.

Using paper, shapes, patterns and colors, we will create mandalas together in this activity. There is no right or wrong way to do it. Making mandalas is about the process more than the product. In Hindu, Tibetan Buddhist, and Dine (Navajo) traditions, mandalas of great beauty are often designed to be temporary, made of colored sand, seeds, or flour, and swept away soon after being completed. When discarded, they allow us to see the beauty of impermanence, and practice letting go of attachments.

Materials
Heavy-duty art or construction paper; several geometric shaped stencils rulers; colored pencils, crayons, markers; meditative music

Step-by-Step Guidelines
Before your circle meets, use a stencil or protractor to draw a large circle on heavy-duty art or construction paper, one piece for each member (or download free mandala templates).

- When you meet, read the activity description and the suggested (or another) poem.
- Ask members to focus on an intention for making their mandala—perhaps ask for insight about a life challenge, to find balance or healing, or to express love or gratitude for someone or something in their life.
- Remind members it is not necessary to be a skilled artist to make a mandala, and to do their best to let go of judgment or self-criticism and express themselves without inhibitions.
- Members should choose their art materials, find a comfortable place to spread out, and begin while maintaining silence.
- Play meditative music throughout the mandala making, pausing periodically to remind members how much time remains.
- When time is up, return to the large group or form triads to share. Prompts might include:
  o *What insights did you gain from this activity?*
  o *Were there any obstacles that got in the way?*
  o *What emotions came up as you were creating your mandala?*
  o *What might it symbolize?*
- Members may choose to save or discard their mandala.

Suggested Resources
Book: Carol Lowell - *Meditative Mandala Making*
Music: Choying Drolma - *Mandala Offering*
　　　　Marta Gomez - *Labios de Cetim*
　　　　Drumspyder - *Bodhi Mandala*
Poetry: Black Elk Speaks - *Circle*
Online: Search for "downloadable mandala templates"

26

Autumn Equinox

Autumn leaves don't fall, they fly.
They take their time and wander on this their only chance to soar. ~Delia Owens

This activity requires more materials and time than most.
Saving this for a retreat day is ideal.

On the Autumn Equinox, in the third week of September in the Northern Hemisphere, day and night are of equal length; the earth is in balance. After this, the days start to become shorter and the nights longer. The light changes, and we might notice a chill in the air. While we can enjoy brisk walks and enjoy autumn's colorful leaves, there are signs that it is time to move from being outwardly focused to going within throughout the fall and winter. Nature scatters the seeds that will generate new growth in the spring.

Sometimes known as the "second harvest," autumn is a time to reflect on the fruits of our labor and the blessings we've received throughout the spring and summer. As we give gratitude for tangible things and the beauty of fall, we also appreciate inner harvests—the special experiences we've enjoyed during the year, and how we have made our way through difficult times.

To celebrate, some ancient cultures built an altar with harvested vegetables, gathered apples and offered them to the Goddess, shared meals, and appreciated their blessings. Throughout the British Isles and Ireland, the Celts braided sheaves from the last harvest into the shape of a woman and honored the "maiden" as the one who helped with the harvest.

In this activity, we make cornhusk maidens to honor the harvest, reflect on our blessings, and begin to prepare for the winter ahead.

Materials

Corn husks (often available at farmers' markets), or bundles of narrow twigs; fall-themed fabric scraps or burlap; twine, ribbons, buttons, beads, pieces of jewelry; glue guns; pinecones, colorful leaves, and squashes for "altar" or center

Step-by-Step Guidelines

- Read one or more poems and the activity description.
- In silence or with music playing, each member will create a "maiden" from corn husks or twigs, and dress her with autumn-themed fabrics, decorative adornments, a piece of jewelry, or other meaningful mementos.
- Ask members to reflect on and give gratitude for any successes or help they have had navigating challenges. Some possible questions to focus on:
  - *What am I grateful for this season?*
  - *What have I harvested from my spring and summer activities?*
  - *Am I in balance—with my work and play, in my relationships, in my body?*
  - *What have I planted that will emerge in spring?*
- After some contemplative time with music, members will name their maiden and thank her for this year's outer or inner harvests.
- Allow time for members to share their maiden's name and the blessings they received this season, and what they learned if they walked through hard or joyful times.
- Suggest members place their maiden in a visible place of honor in their home until Winter Solstice and ask for her guidance throughout the season if challenges arise.

Suggested Resources

Book: Luisah Teish - *Jump Up: Good Times Throughout the Seasons With Celebrations from Around the World.*

Music: Libana - *Autumn Time*
Yenne Lee - *Autumn Leaves* (guitar solo)
Cheryl Wheeler - *When Fall Comes to New England*

Poetry: Wendell Berry - *The Wild Geese*
Jeanne Lohmann - *What the Day Gives*

AUTUMN

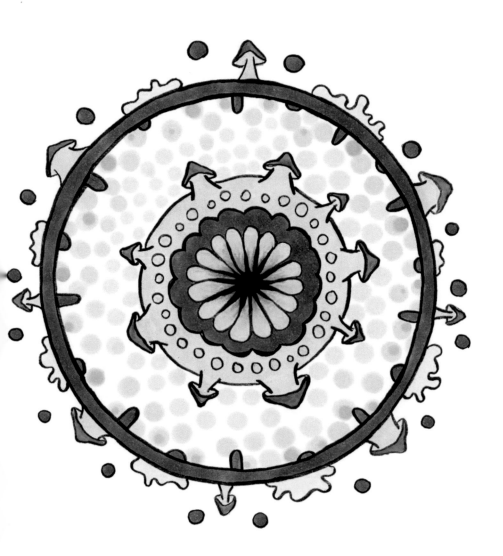

27

Inside Out

. . . the actual task is to integrate the two threads of one's life . . .
the within and the without. ~Pierre Teilhard de Chardin

There is a wise saying about not comparing our insides to other people's outsides. Sometimes we show a different face to the world than what is inside, especially if we have a history of others not listening to our needs or refusing to accept our feelings or beliefs as we grew up. There can be a gap between who we are, and who we present to the world to be accepted or fit in.

Depending on the size of our women's groups and their purpose, and how long they have been meeting, being genuine and disclosing our authentic selves can be intimidating. Showing vulnerability might have been, or still might be, unsafe in our families, at work, or in our social circles. One of the most beautiful things about women's groups is that *we can discover how freeing it is* to let other people know more about what is going on inside. We learn that vulnerability is not weakness but is one of the best measures of our courage.

Also, it can be helpful to hear how other women view their inner world. This activity lets others, and perhaps us, see more of our true selves, and can diminish our fears about being more open and vulnerable with others.

Materials

A paper grocery bag or shoebox; magazines with pictures to cut out; glue or tape

Step-by-Step Guidelines

- Ask members to reflect on who they are on the outside, and who they are on the inside. They can cut out words and pictures from magazines that reflect their *inner* world—feelings, thoughts, identities, desires—and those that represent their *outer* world or what they present to others.

- Ask them to affix the outer pictures and words on the outside of the paper bag or shoebox, and to place the inner pictures and words inside the bag or box.

- Allow time for members one by one to share their outside items and inside items with the circle, or in triads for a large group.

Note: Variations on this activity are for members to focus on how they are on the inside and outside right now in the present moment (rather than in general), or to choose pictures and words that reflect what they want to cultivate in their inner world and what they want to convey in the outer world in the future.

Suggested Resources

Movie: Disney/Pixar - *Inside Out*

Music: India.Arie - *I Choose*

Radiant Children - *Sky Mind*

28

Three Desires

If we are looking for life and love and openness and growth,
we are likely to find them. ~Madeleine L'Engle

Women who express strong desires are sometimes perceived negatively. If we desire to be in high leadership roles, we are "too ambitious." If we want to be paid the same as men in sports or entertainment, we are "too competitive." If we have strong sexual desires, we might be shamed for it. Sometimes even our mothers or grandmothers gave us subtle negative messages about wanting too much or seeking too much attention. Yet some of our greatest teachers tell us our problem is not having desire; it is that our desires are too small.

The original root of the word desire comes from the Latin *de sidere*, or "from the stars." Desire is not so much grasping for something, as it is asking for what the stars may bring: *May I be happy; May I experience abundance; May I find a kind and healthy partner; May I have meaningful work.*

What if we could be as visionary, whimsical, or *desirous* as we want? This activity gives us the freedom to express whatever our hearts desire *without limitations*, and to silence the voice that whispers it's better to play it safe and not risk disappointment.

Materials

A few small empty boxes; small slips of paper and pens

Step-by-Step Guidelines

- Before the meeting, ask members to bring a small empty box to the meeting. Bring a few extra boxes for those who forget.

- At the meeting, ask everyone *to be as bold as possible* and list at least 10 of their heart's desires, even if they seem like impossible fantasies. Having said this, suggest that women focus on desires they have some power over. "*I desire to win the lottery.*" could be reframed as "*I desire financial abundance.*"

- Play music and allow enough time for everyone to complete their lists. Volunteers can read their entire lists aloud for fun.

- Ask everyone to choose three desires from their list to consider further—desires that perhaps they are ready to take a step toward fulfilling. Members will write the three desires on slips of paper. Women can choose to share their three desires out loud (or not) before placing them in their box, which should be kept in a special place in their home.

- Ask if any members would like to share a concrete step they are ready to take to fulfill one desire.

Suggested Resources

Music: Cesaria Evora - *Sodade*

Alicia Keys & Brandi Carlile - *A Beautiful Noise*

Linda Ronstadt - *When You Wish Upon a Star*

Bebe Rexha - *You Can't Stop the Girl*

Poetry: Alice Walker - *Desire*

John O'Donohue - *For Longing*

29

Discovering Animal Allies

I pray to the birds because they remind me of what I love rather than what I fear.
And at the end of my prayers, they teach me how to listen.
~Terry Tempest Williams

A nimal allies are animals with whom we feel a meaningful connection. Throughout recorded history, groups and individuals from cultures around the world have formed deep affinities with animals. An indigenous clan or tribe might be connected to Bear or Wolf, or a person might be named after or have a lifelong totem of a deer or eagle. In mythology, folk tales, and fiction, animal allies have been represented by a *fylgja* in Norse mythology, the Patronus in *Harry Potter*, or the daemon in *The Golden Compass*.

In our own lives, we can choose (or be called by) animal allies who teach us, help us grow, or are at our side when we are troubled. They may have traits or behaviors we want to embody. We can call on them when we are trying to develop a particular characteristic like strength, patience, wisdom, playfulness, or empathy.

Each year in December or January, we can focus attention on discovering an animal ally for the coming year. The animal almost always makes its presence known—appearing in notable ways in the outdoors, in images that repeatedly show up, or in a dream. Once the animal is chosen (or as many believe, chooses *us*) we set aside time during the year to learn more about the animal. We might bring pictures of the animal into our home, have it represented in our jewelry and clothing, or draw, sketch, or collage about the animal—all to discover what the animal might have to teach us, and why it might have arrived in our lives at that particular time.

Throughout the year, we can continue to consider and benefit from our animal's lessons. Several times sea turtles have come to Billie during guided imagery journeys or dreams, and she has been encouraged to embody the turtles' characteristics of being able to protect themselves yet remain gentle, not "push the river," and stay calm in turbulent waters.

One-year bees visited Cassi everywhere she went. She adopted the bee as her animal for the next year, bringing bee imagery into her house, reading books like *The Secret Life of Bees*, watching movies about bees, and even taking a daylong beekeeping seminar. She investigated them throughout the year, learning how bees work together as a team, how the queen bee is a servant leader, and how bees "dance" to communicate with one another.

In this activity, we choose an animal to work with in our own lives and share what we must learn from the animal and/or what it might symbolize for us.

Materials
Medicine Cards or other animal cards; magazines with animal photos

Step-by-Step Guidelines

- About a month before your group meets, ask members to notice animals that cross their path, or appear in dreams and printed materials. Suggest they not judge the animal that comes to them, but let whatever arises be the one, whether real or mythical. Tell them not to worry if no animal appears, because they will be able to find an animal during your meeting.

- When you meet, open the circle by having members who don't have an animal to work with draw a Medicine Card from the deck, or from animal pictures you provide.

- You may also lead a guided visualization or play a recorded one (see Suggested Resources) in which they can be guided through an encounter with the animal they have already chosen or find their animal.

- When everyone has found their animal, volunteers can read aloud information about the animal in the *Medicine Cards* book or another online resource, and/or share their thoughts about the animal who chose them.

Suggested Resources
Book: Erika Buenaflor - *Animal Medicine: A Curanderismo Guide to Shapeshifting, Journeying, and Connecting with Animal Allies*
Deck: Jamie Sams, David Carson, and Angela C. Wernecke - *Medicine Cards*
Music: Brooke Medicine Eagle - *Wishi Ta*
Poetry: Diane Glancy - *The Eight 0 Five*
Online: Search for "animal symbolism"

30

Making Hand Sculptures

To receive everything, one must open one's hands and give. ~Taisen Deshimaru

This activity requires more materials and time than most.
Saving it for a retreat day is ideal.

Hands are one of the most often symbolized parts of the human body. They represent giving and receiving love and blessings, strength and protection, and service to others. Universally, hands are associated with human connection and can communicate our unspoken feelings. Handprints are some of the oldest cave drawings. In many cultures and religions, hand gestures symbolize divine power. Hindus and Buddhists use more than 500 meaningful hand gestures (*mudras*) in dance and rituals.

Often hands are purified or embellished before ceremonies or initiations. "Sculpting" them can be a meditative experience, a process of intuitive discovery, or simply a fun art project.

This activity, in which we make and embellish a plaster cast of one of our hands, works best when members take turns working in dyads. Each finger on our sculpted hand can represent something different: areas of our life we want to focus on, key aspects of ourselves, things we want more of in our life, experiences we want to remember, people we love, things we are ready to let go of, or places we have been or want to go.

If nothing comes to mind, we can create and decorate our hand sculpture intuitively, without any specific plan. Later we can research the cultural symbolic meanings of each hand or each finger and see what came forth from our subconscious during the activity. Was the hand open or closed? Did its gesture indicate love, anger, or fear? What might it mean?

Materials

Plaster gauze (available at medical supply stores) cut into small strips; petroleum jelly (Vaseline); bowls of warm water; old towels; acrylic paints, brushes; glue; printed pictures, symbols, words, designs; small stones, cords, feathers, and beads for embellishing the hands

Step-by-Step Guidelines

- Open the circle by asking each woman to become quiet, find a partner, lay towels down, fill their bowl with warm water, and cut their plaster gauze strips (about 40-50, three inches long and two inches wide).

- Share the activity description and if you'd like, play one of the instructional YouTube videos.

- To create hand sculptures:
  - Members will coat one of their partner's hands and wrist generously in Vaseline.
  - Dip plaster strips in water, and apply strips to the whole hand, top and palm, and around the fingers, like a glove. Keep the hand very still as the strips are being applied, in whatever position you'd like. Smooth the first layer so that the plaster becomes like liquid and the gauze strips blend into one another.
  - Add 3-4 layers of strips, smoothing them as needed. The hand sculpture will harden. It may become warm during the hardening process.
  - When partially dry, members will ease the mold off their hands. They may need help cutting a slit at the wrist so the mold will come off. Cover the slit with more wet plaster strips to hide it.
  - Sit in silence or with music for 5-10 minutes while the hand sculptures mostly dry.
  - Members will then decorate their hands with paints and embellishments.
  - Ask each woman to share their experience and the meaning of their hands.

Note: An easier version of this activity is for members to simply trace around one hand on heavy paper and decorate it. A more ambitious version is to make a plaster mask on the face and see what or who comes forward.

Suggested Resources
Music: Jewel - *Hands*
          Sherene - *Grandma's Hands*
Poetry: Ellen Bass - *To Praise*
          Anne Sullivan Macy - *Hands*
          Margaret Atwood - *You Begin*
Online: Search YouTube for "plaster gauze hand mask-making"

31

Mapping Our Lives

you will be lost and unlost, over and over again. relax love.
You were meant to be this glorious. epic. story.
~niyyirah waheed

As the old saying goes, *the map is not the territory,* but if you have ever tried traveling in a new landscape without one, you likely discovered how useful they can be. While we have all kinds of stories about how our lives have unfolded, it can be powerful to use visuals rather than narratives to help us understand the journey that brought us to this point.

Learning more about where we have come from can shed light on where we are going, and what we might want to leave behind or take with us. Like the great explorers of the past who walked all day and drew pictures of the major landmarks they encountered, dangers along the way, and resources or vistas that might warrant a return visit, mapping our lives can be illuminating.

In this activity, we weave together a visual map of important moments or seasons in our lives. We can learn more about where we stand in the landscape of our world, and maybe even become a cartographer of our future journey.

Materials

Pens, markers, crayons; blank notebooks or drawing/newsprint paper; hard backing for drawing on papers (such as a notebook, cardboard, or table)

Step-by-Step Guidelines

- Share these suggestions or use a guided visualization to help members imagine their map before they create it.
- Create a map of your life starting from when you were born to today. You can symbolize your life journey with: a winding road, a hiking trail, a pirate's map, a journey around the world, a galaxy or star map, or a neighborhood or city map. Use the metaphor that comes to mind.
- You may want to add the major landmarks of your life—when your family moved, when a sibling was born, graduations, marriages, childbirths, loss of loved ones, traumas, and peak experiences. It can be helpful to break it into seven-year periods.
- Members can also be more specific and create:
  o A professional map—charting the course of your career
  o A spirituality map—showing your life-long spiritual practices, communities, interests, and beliefs
  o A relationship map—reflecting on your romantic interests and how they have shaped your life
  o An inspirational people and mentors map—highlighting the helpers and guides you've encountered along your journey
- Suggest that members use as many pictures, symbols, and metaphors as they can; use words sparingly; imagine it as a fairy tale or a myth; and let their visual imagination rather than their mental descriptions lead the way.
- Allow time for members to share their maps with the group.

Suggested Resources

Book: Jill K. Berry - *Personal Geographies*

Music: k.d. lang - *The Valley*
           Indigo Girls - *Get Out the Map*
                    ~niyyirah waheed

Poetry: Lucille Clifton - *i am running into a new year*
           Mary Oliver - *The Journey*
           Ursula K. LeGuin - *Come to Dust*

32
Healing Ceremony

Barn's burnt down, now I can see the moon. ~Mzuta Masahide

None of us get through life without experiencing some difficult moments or seasons. Each of us has wounds and traumas, whether physical, emotional, or spiritual. In modern mainstream, masculine, mechanistic societies, healing is typically attributed to physicians and pharmaceuticals. We as women are expected to be passive recipients.

But throughout millennia, women have been the primary healers. Even today, the female-dominated nursing profession is the unsung backbone of the medical system. In women's groups since the beginning of recorded history, healing ceremonies have eased our pain and restored our wholeness in body, mind, and spirit. In many cultures, women would gather during their monthly menses for healing and restoration (with the shadow, of course, of women being banished during these times as *unclean*).

When something happens that unravels the threads of our daily lives, women's healing ceremonies can allow us to rely on the power of sisterhood to deal with physical pain, to grieve, or to move on from painful memories and losses. We can find profound ease from current difficulties and past hurts by participating in a healing ceremony in our women's groups.

Every one of us can feel empowered to direct positive healing intentions toward another, even if we are not trained healers. The key is to imagine the healing energy that is present in the universe, in nature, in our ancestors, and as women to flow through us. We can allow this energy to be conveyed through our own kindness and compassion toward our sisters in the group. When we direct healing in this way, we are not depleted, but strengthened.

Materials

A small piece of flammable and biodegradable paper (about 1/4 of an 8.5x11 sheet) for each group member; 6-inch lengths of natural twine or string; pens

Step-by-Step Guidelines

- Ask each member to reflect on a current pain or painful memory, and to recognize how every other woman in the group is there to offer healing energy to her. Ask members to imagine a harm they feel they have the strength and readiness to face and release.
- Ask members to write a word, phrase, or symbol that represents the hurt or memory, and secure the paper into a bundle or scroll with a ribbon or string.

Three options for continuing the healing ceremony:

- In a small, safe fire, either in a fireproof container outdoors or in a fireplace indoors, ask each woman to burn her bundle, while members send compassion and positive energy toward her highest good.
- Find a large tree in the outdoors, or go to the ocean, and ask each woman to throw her bundle high into the tree or into the ocean, saying out loud *I release you*, echoed by the other members saying *We release you*.
- Ask each woman to sit or lie down in the center of the circle. With her permission, each member can put their hands on her hands, feet, knees, shoulders, and head, and attend to clearing her body, mind, and spirit from any unnecessary suffering or leftover stuck places. Members can do the same without touching the person, by visualizing or sending healing energy through their intention.

Suggested Resources

Book: Shamini Jain - *Healing Ourselves: Biofield Science and the Future of Health*

Music: Carrie Newcomer - *Abide*
            Yair Levi and Shai Sol - *El Na Rafa Na La*
            Ann Reed - *I Will Be There for You*

Poetry: Mary Oliver - *Heavy*

33

Building Resilience

I've put up with too much, too long, and now I'm just too intelligent, too powerful, too beautiful, too sure of who I am finally to deserve anything less.
~Sandra Cisneros

Resilience is the ability to recover from or adjust to challenges or change. So, how do we bounce back from difficult times or stressful changes in our lives? How do we turn to our core strengths and stay grounded when under pressure? How do we become resilient women?

Resilience is developed by encountering experiences throughout our lives that are just challenging enough, but not too overwhelming or traumatic. This kind of "optimal stress" is kind of like building muscle by lifting weights. We stretch ourselves just past our comfort zone, followed by a period of rest and renewal, and over time we increase our strength.

Even when experiences feel way beyond our ability to handle them, with enough support and self-care these can build resilience too, as opposed to either weakening us or hardening us. Practicing self-care and adding to our internal resources are crucial. These can include learning to be flexible around things we can't control, having the ability to stay awake and present, focusing on what we can learn from the situation, and finding humor when possible. Practices like meditation, writing, being in nature, body-based breathing, tai chi, qi gong, or yoga calm the mind through repeated practice and change the way our mind functions.

In other words, we build resilience walking through difficulties throughout our lives. We develop coping skills and the discernment to use them effectively. This activity introduces a practice of mindfulness, which research shows lowers stress and allows us to stay present in the moment, rather than being hijacked by frustrating or hurtful experiences. Practicing mindfulness can help us develop the resilience and spirit to handle the challenges of everyday life.

Materials

None needed

Step-by-Step Guidelines

- Ask members to find a comfortable position and to maintain silence during this activity. As much as possible remove any distractions from the room. You can play music softly if you'd like.
- Read the activity description and the Rumi poem.
- Suggest members pay attention to the breath, slowly counting to four on the inhalations and six on the exhalations. Explain that if the mind wanders, simply return to the breath and be present in the moment, letting go of the past and thoughts of the future, and noticing what appears in their mental, physical, and emotional experiences without evaluations or judgment.
- Ask members to consider these questions in silence:
  - *How resilient are you when a big change happens in your life?*
  - *What is your strongest inner resource?*
  - *What ways of coping would help you better handle disappointments?*
- Ask members to share what they experienced during this activity.

Suggested Resources

Music: Audra Day - *Rise Up*
Purity of Mind - *Lotus Sutra from Beyond* (album)
Mary J. Blige - *Mighty River*
Rising Appalachia - *Resilient*

Poetry: Jelaluddin Rumi - *The Guest House*
Jeannette Encinias - *Beneath the Sweater and the Skin*

Online: Search for Sharon Salzberg - *Lovingkindness Meditation*
Free guided meditations by James Baraz are at
awakeningjoy.info

34

Redefining Giving Up

There is a difference between giving up and
knowing that you've had enough. ~Anonymous

In some situations, the way to solve a problem is to *stop participating* in the problem. At times, the more we keep trying to force things to get better, like staying in a job, friendship, bowling team, or board of directors that isn't right for us, the more we become enmeshed in the problem.

We may have heard from a parent or other authority figure "*You should always finish what you started.*" or "*You can't be a quitter.*" To give up meant we weren't living up to someone else's expectations, or to our own *shoulds.* Even dropping out of an activity like an art class or a book club that isn't as nourishing or enjoyable as we thought it would be can cause us to feel like we are letting ourselves down.

On the other hand, some of us drop out of things pretty often. We have trouble following through with commitments, and may "quit before the miracle," rather than pushing ourselves through the learning phases. This kind of giving up needs redefining too. We may want to course-correct, adjust, or jump tracks rather than indulging our desire to prematurely give up, or spiral into shame or rebellion.

Danielle LaPorte calls it "Reframing Quit" in her book *The Fire Starter Sessions*: "It's not so much quitting as . . . stopping, ceasing, retiring, putting it to rest, letting it fly, moving on, phasing out, bringing to a conclusion, taking a bow, changing course, clarifying, focusing, perfecting, shifting, trading up."

Sometimes, giving up is about honoring our feelings, improving our mental health, and being our authentic selves. This activity helps us reframe giving up and helps us become aware of where we need to take a self-affirming action.

Materials
Personal journals; pens or pencils

Step-by-Step Guidelines

- Ask members to share their beliefs about giving up or quitting. What messages did they receive from their parents, authority figures, or peers?

- Ask members to get into dyads and share for five minutes each about 1) a time in their life that they gave up or quit, and wished they hadn't, and 2) a time that they ended their participation in something and found it was the right decision—one that was necessary or led to greater thriving.

- Ask women to take about ten minutes to write responses to these prompts:
  o *Whom did you have to disappoint to make your decision, and how did that feel?*
  o *Did your desire to quit cause anxiety?*
  o *Did doubt about your abilities, perfectionism, or being attached to a specific outcome delay your decision?*

- Allow time for members to share some of their written responses, and how they feel about their decision now.

Suggested Resources
Books: Danielle LaPorte - *The Fire-Starter Sessions: A Soulful and Practical Guide to Creating Success on Your Own Terms*
Glennon Doyle - *Untamed*
Music: Carol Woods & Timothy Mitchum - *Let It Be* (Across the Universe Version)
Luba - *Let It Go*
Chiwoniso - *Listen to the Breeze*
Marja Helena Fjellheim Mortensson & Katarina Barruk - *Mattarahkku*

35

Joy Jars

Joy is the best makeup. ~Anne Lamott

On the days we just feel *blah* it is hard to appreciate the wonders of life and the joy they have brought us. Turning our attention toward gratitude, love, and joy can counteract the negative thinking patterns that might appear on days we feel low.

It is important to purposely attend to and amplify positive emotions and states of mind. Research shows that savoring or being intentionally mindful of positive experiences leads to greater happiness, less depression, and more life satisfaction. The work of scientist Barbara Fredrickson shows that spending time with our positive emotions like serenity, hope, awe, inspiration, and love broadens our mindset and builds our resources, leading to an upward spiral of novel and creative ideas, healthier actions, and good relationships. Paying attention to what brings us happiness, be it something little or profound, is a good daily habit.

Filling a *Joy Jar* helps us remember and return to simple pleasures that lift our spirits on those days when we are feeling uneasy. In this activity, making our Joy Jars together is a creative and fun way to plan ahead for down days. We can fill the jar with happy memories and things that bring us joy, and add one or two more any time we want, savoring the little fulfilling things that make life sweet.

Materials

Paper and pens; medium-sized jars or vases—one for each member; art papers; glue; beads, markers, stickers, nature materials

Step-by-Step Guidelines

- Before your meeting, ask members to bring a jar or vase and art materials to the meeting.
- At the meeting, open the circle by reading a poem or two.
- Ask a group member to read the activity description out loud.
- Play upbeat music while members gather their materials and decorate their jars.
- Ask members to write uplifting actions, situations, things, or memories on slips of paper, taking a moment to savor each one, and place them in their jars.
- Allow time for members to share some of their joyful memories or actions with the group.
- Mention that it is fine for members to "borrow" others' ideas and add them to their jars.
- Play some joyful music and encourage members to dance together.

Suggested Resources

Books: Shonda Rhimes - *Year of Yes: How to Dance It Out, Stand in the Sun, and Be Your Own Person*
Sylvia Boorstein - *Happiness Is an Inside Job: Practicing for a Joyful Life*
Music: Sona Jobarteh - *Jarabi*
Madeleine Peyroux - *Getting Some Fun Out of Life*
The Mamas and the Papas - *Dancing in the Street*
Mary Chapin Carpenter - *I Feel Lucky*
Poetry: Caitlin Ju - *Little Joys: A Poem*
Jane Kenyon - *Happiness*

36

Drumming Practice

The drum connects our hearts to the heartbeat of Mother Earth.
~Anonymous

Drumming has been a deep feminine practice throughout history. Women were often the drummers during sacred rituals. When our women's groups drum together, we create a heartfelt connection that strengthens our bond with each other. Adding rattles, shakers, sticks, spoons, or clapping can add to celebratory drum circles, or when clearing out old energy to make way for the new.

Sustained drumming can lead to an altered or expanded state of awareness. Some research shows that our bodies physically entrain or get "in-sync" with the drumbeat, leading to a deep meditative, ecstatic, or transcendent state. Drumming can take us beyond our small self, or our personal story. It can quiet our minds and bring forward images and perceptions relevant to ongoing personal work.

When a confusing or troubling situation arises, drumming can help us access insights our logical minds might miss. The drumbeat can walk us through grief, important rites of passage, or ecstatic celebrations. Drumming can be used in healing rituals, for removing blocks or obstacles, or for empowerment. And sometimes, we drum just to drum.

Drumming together can help our group focus on an intention, offer prayers, grieve, heal, or mark a meaningful celebration. This activity can also help strengthen bonds among the group or move the group out of "thinking" and into "being."

Materials

Personal journals; drums, rattles, or other noisemakers

Step-by-Step Guidelines

- Before the group meets, ask members to bring a drum if possible, or another drum-like "instrument" or a rattle. Self-made instruments are welcome, like a cylindrical oatmeal container or a recycled container with dried beans inside.

- At the meeting, ask members to individually set an intention— a specific prayer, expression of joy or gratitude, request for healing, guidance with a problem, or to simply be open to whatever arises. The group can also collectively drum for a purpose, for example, to pray for the highest good for a member going through a difficult time, or to mark the occasion of a graduation, birth, death, or other.

- Designate a drum leader who will establish and hold the rhythm. You might also find a local person who has experience with drumming circles to guest facilitate.

- Establish a time frame for the drumming—20 to 30 minutes is ideal.

- When a strong beat has been established members will join in when they feel the rhythm. Suggest that the women close their eyes and imagine a heartbeat that comes from the center of Mother Earth. Suggest that they pay attention to any entities (perhaps ancestors or animals) that join them during their drumming "journey."

- After the drumming, allow time for members to journal and/or share with the group what they experienced during the drumming.

Suggested Resources

Books: Layne Redmond - *When the Drummers Were Women*
       Mickey Hart with Jay Stevens - *Drumming at the Edge of Magic*

Music: Shamanic Drumming World - *Shamanic Meditation Journey*
       Marla Leigh - *Frame Drum Practice*
       Ulali-Mahk Jchi - *Heartbeat Drum Song*

37

Let's Get Physical

Life is a terrific gym. Every situation is an opportunity to practice.
~Sylvia Boorstein

Many of us have overactive minds. Our very busy minds can assault us with unwanted thoughts and feelings, making it difficult to consciously make choices that promote better health and happiness. "Monkey mind" chatter about the state of the world or an ongoing personal problem may interfere with our ability to live each day fully. It can feel as though we are centered an inch or two behind our foreheads most of the time.

Learning to pause and move our center of gravity from our minds into our bodies can help us stay awake and grounded during stressful times. Embodiment, in this sense, means fully inhabiting our bodies, or locating our awareness in our belly and heart as much as in our head. Assuming specific poses or postures in yoga or other contemplative movement practices help us reside more fully in our bodies. We can also use hand gestures or movements to ground us in our physical being.

This activity gives us tools to free our minds from thinking of work that needs to be done, and to stop worrying about the future or the past. Familiar gestures like putting our hands on our heart or on our cheeks for several breaths allow us to acknowledge the tension in our body and release it, and several other gestures shift consciousness and free the mind.

Materials

None needed

Step-by-Step Guidelines

- Read the activity description. You might play soft music during this activity.
- Ask members to try the following, allowing a minute or two for each one. You might go through them each silently, one by one, or you might ask members to share what comes up for them after each one. You can do this in a small group, or in dyads.

  o *Tightly clench and slowly release your hands.*
  o *Tightly clench and slowly release your whole body.*
  o *Pause at the end of an out-breath for several seconds, placing a hand over your heart.*
  o *With your other hand, trace the infinity symbol (a horizontal "8") in the air.*
  o *Cross your arms over your chest until you are hugging your shoulders.*
  o *Gradually spread your arms as wide as you can.*
  o *Lower your head in a bow, palms of hands together.*
  o *Extend your hands with the palms up.*
  o *Hold your hands on your cheeks.*

- Ask members to share how they felt moved by, or responded to, any of the gestures.
- A meaningful way to end this activity is to offer a prayer bow or *namaste* (a form of respectfully greeting and honoring a person by placing the palms together with the thumbs close to the body and slightly bowing) to each member of the circle.

Suggested Resources

Book: Gertrud Hirschi - *Mudras: Yoga in Your Hands*
Music: Yaima - *The Sacred*

38

Speaking With Ancestors

. . . our grandparents are the dreamers and storytellers
from whose imagination we arrive here. ~Joy Harjo

Many of the world's cultural and spiritual traditions believe our ancestors are available to help guide us. They stand behind us as we face difficult challenges, act as cosmic cheerleaders in our life's journey, and can hold us accountable to our personal and cultural integrity. In this view, our ancestors are not limited by the normal limitations of space and time. They can assist us whether living or dead, across great distances, or if they lived long ago.

In some cultures, the ancestors are a part of everyday life. You might consult a long-dead grandmother for help cooking a stew as easily as looking at a cookbook. Whether you believe this literally or not, even *imagining* such figures can be a useful exercise to gain strength or feel less alone. When we are making a big life change, or walking through a rough period, we might call upon our ancestors to lend us strength.

Ancestors can include people who were actually related to us, people from our cultural or ethnic background, or people who were part of a social movement we are a part of (such as our feminist ancestors or our queer ancestors). When standing up for civil rights, we might call on ancestors such as Dr. Martin Luther King Jr., Rosa Parks, Harriet Tubman, or Sojourner Truth to stand behind us.

At times our ancestors can be problematic, having been complicit in the oppression of others, passing on addictive patterns, or carrying forward intergenerational trauma. Ancestor work can help us to become aware of biological, cultural, and behavioral legacies we might wish to heal and release, or familial patterns we may wish to break in our own lifetimes.

This activity encourages us to reflect upon our ancestors and to call on their wisdom and support.

Materials

Personal journals or paper and pens; colored pencils or markers (optional)

Step-by-Step Guidelines

- Ask members to sit or lie down, close their eyes, and listen to this guided meditation:

    o *Breathe deeply, allowing the breath to bring oxygen to your entire body, imagining it as though your breath was reaching all the way to the top of your head and the tips of your fingers and toes. (Pause) Feel your body and your awareness in this present moment.*

    o *Reflect on an issue that is troubling you, a change you are making, or an intention for your future. Allow that issue, change, or intention to fill your awareness. What do you think about it? What do you feel about it? How does your body respond to it?*

    o *Now imagine you feel a person or group of people who lived before you— your ancestors—standing behind you or supporting you in facing this issue, change or intention. They may be shoulder to shoulder with you. Invite them to join you.*

    o *Ask the person or people who they are. (Pause) Ask them what you need to know about the situation (Pause). Ask if they have any gifts, they might bring to the situation for you (Pause). Ask them if they can help you address it (Pause). Let them know what kind of help you need, specifically. You might ask, "How do I need to be in this situation?" (Pause). They may have a specific word, symbol, or gift for you.*

    o *You can thank your ancestors, and you can also choose to reject any advice or gifts. At times, ancestors will appear who are carrying old harmful patterns. If this should happen let them know you choose to heal and release them, saying something like, "I no longer want to be part of the lineage of (dishonesty, hatred, fear, addiction). I wish for your healing, and I release any and all bonds I have to you or you to me."*

    o *(After a pause of a few minutes) Please bring your attention now back to your body and your breathing. Feel the ground or seat beneath you and take three deep breaths. Rub your hands together, stretch, and open your eyes.*

- Ask members to write notes or draw sketches about their experience, then break into dyads or triads to share for 10-15 minutes. When they return to the circle, ask if anyone wants to share something with the larger group.

Suggested Resources

Music: Ricki Byers Beckwith - *In the Land of I Am*

Windsong Martin - *Mother I Feel You*

Ann Reed - *Where the Earth Is Round*

Our Native Daughters - *You're Not Alone*

Poetry: Nikita Gill - *Ancestors*

Online: Luisah Teish: *Honoring Ancestors* on the Earth Medicine Alliance Voices of the Earth YouTube Channel

39

Winter Solstice

As the winter stars appear in the darkness of the heavens, may
they along with us witness the renewal of hope in the darkest night.
~Celtic devotional

Winter Solstice is celebrated in almost every culture around the world. Midwinter festivals include the Norse Yuletide, Saturnalia in ancient Rome, Dong Zhi in China, Shab-e Yalda in Iran, Shalako in the Zuni Pueblo people, Christmas, Hanukkah, African American Kwanzaa and many more. For thousands of years, people have gathered near the time when the night is longest, and the day is shortest to tend the fire through the night and celebrate the return of the light. In the Southern Hemisphere, this occurs in June.

Just like the seeds buried in the cool depth of the earth prepare to emerge with the warmth of the sun, it is a time for us to discover the power of stillness, quietly contemplate and release the past year, and prepare to symbolically be "reborn." It's a time to express gratitude for the gifts and blessings we have received throughout the year, to discard the old, and to prepare for the promise of self-renewal in the coming year.

Winter is a good time for reflection. It reminds us that deep rest is essential for all living things. It is a fruitful darkness in which the seeds of new ideas can gradually develop and prepare to emerge. Billie's women's group that has met for 20 years always finds this simple ritual one of the most meaningful of the year. We feel the stirrings of new parts of ourselves ready to emerge, and others ready to be resurrected. We remember that in the darkest time, the light within never dies.

Materials

Votive candles and lighter; small flashlight for leader to read the questions; seasonal greenery and berries for the altar; special foods; music

Step-by-Step Guidelines

- Before you meet, ask all members to bring a votive candle and a favorite delicacy to your solstice gathering. Create a festive "altar" or table with seasonal materials.
- At the meeting, play soft seasonal music and read the activity description.
- Turn out the lights and allow a few minutes for members to experience the darkness in silence, then to reflect on these questions:
  - *What were your greatest gifts from last year?*
  - *What was the darkest time of the year for you, the most challenging time?*
  - *What did you learn from it?*
  - *What are you ready to release from your life at this time?*
- Allow time for each member to share her responses.
- Ask members to reflect on these questions and play another piece of music if you wish:
  - *What would you like to bring into the coming year to enhance your life?*
  - *How will your life be richer and more meaningful?*
- Ask each member, one by one, to light their votive candle, and share their responses.
- When all members have shared their hopes and intentions for the coming year, all the candles can be extinguished, and the lights turned on.
- Celebrate the return of the light with music and sharing of food and beverages.

Suggested Resources

Music: William Ackerman/Windham Hill - *A Winter Solstice*
          Pentatonix - *Dance of the Sugar Plum Fairy*
          Melissa Manchester - *There's Still My Joy*
          Patty Griffin - *Heavenly Day*
          Putamayo - *Joy to the World* (album)

Poetry: Mary Oliver - *Starlings in Winter*
         Elizabeth Alexander - *Praise Song for the Day*

WINTER

40

Letters to Ourselves

You can be a thousand different women. It's your choice which one you want to be.
It's about freedom and sovereignty. You celebrate who you are.
~Salma Hayek

Setting intentions for the coming year is a key part of many New Year's rituals. Different from New Year's resolutions, which are sometimes unrealistic promises, intentions are a way of sharing with others and ourselves what we hope we will prioritize and create in the coming year.

We reflect on our intentions for the year in this activity and write letters to ourselves meant to be opened in July. Often, we forget completely about the letter, and it comes as a welcome surprise in the mail—an unexpected reminder of our intentions at the beginning of the year. It is a good opportunity to reflect on how our intentions have manifested, to explore if and how they have changed, or to recommit to aligning our actions with our intentions and values.

Materials

Journal or paper and pens; an assortment of stationery or paper for letter writing; stamped envelopes; pens, pencils, and colored markers; stickers and/or washi tape

Step-by-Step Guidelines

- Ask members to write their priorities and intentions for the coming year. Suggest that they avoid creating a list of New Year's resolutions, but instead choose four or five simply stated goals such as "spend time in nature," "eat more whole foods," "move my body daily," "get closer to my granddaughter," or "increase my income."

- Ask members to consider what they would like to remind themselves of, with respect to these goals, six months into the future. How might they be an encouraging cheerleader to their six-months-in-the-future self? Do they want to express gratitude to themselves in the future? Send themselves a gift certificate or a DIY "coupon" for a day of self-care?

- Distribute the writing materials and ask everyone to write a letter to herself.

- Some possible prompts:
  - *I'm writing to remind you that . . .*
  - *I believe in you because . . .*
  - *I'm grateful for everything you've done to . . .*
  - *My gift to you is . . .*

- Members will decorate their letters and self-address an envelope; they will entrust their letter to the leader or another trustworthy member to be mailed to them exactly six months in the future. As leader, put a note in your calendar to send the letters or remind others to send their letters.

Suggested Resources

Music: Stevie Wonder - *Signed, Sealed, Delivered*
        Joe Cocker - *The Letter*
        Madame Gandhi - *The Future Is Female*
Poetry: Derek Wolcott - *Love After Love*

41

Recharging in Nature

Into the forest I go
to lose my mind and find my soul.
~John Muir

Silence and nature provide an environment where we can do inner work and nurture our spirit. Things as simple as the sky, the stars, or the buzzing of bees can bring solace, joy, and spiritual meaning into our lives.

Sometimes the only thing that can match the intensity of the emotions we feel inside is the beauty and vastness of nature. When we are in a season of flow in our lives, the mountains, the deep forests, the waters, or the desert, or even a park or our backyard can energize us and bring forth a sense of awe, gratitude, and the unity of all creation. When we are depressed, depleted, or joyless, we can go out into nature to find peace and regain a sense of ease within ourselves. The earth can absorb our tears, compost our grief, recharge our batteries, and help us remember who we are meant to be.

Many of us live rushing through work, relationships, and commitments. The rhythms found in nature are mostly slow to medium—in the waves of the ocean, the wind in the trees, the gently falling rain. When we lose touch with the rhythms of nature, we become unbalanced. Spending time outdoors can help us get our groove back. This activity lets us experience the gifts of time, silence, and regeneration in nature.

Materials
Personal journals or pen and paper

Step-by-Step Guidelines
- To prepare for this activity, request that members spend one hour or more outdoors in silence at least once before your next meeting. Ask them to observe what they experience, and to note their thoughts, feelings, or body sensations in their journals.
- At the meeting, play music and share selected poems about nature.
- Ask each woman to share her solo experience in nature.
- Discussion questions might be:
  o *What places in nature do you (or do you think you would) love the most—mountains, waters, deserts, or woods—and why?*
  o *What did you see that could be a source of creative inspiration for you?*
  o *Where did you experience peace, awe, or joy?*
  o *How might you bring more of nature's gifts into your life?*
- Ask members to state what element of nature they feel most connected to, using an "I am . . ." statement, such as *I am a leaf,* or *I am a sun,* or *I am lightning.*

Suggested Resources
Music: Libana - *A River of Birds*
         Sara Bareilles - *Saint Honesty*
         Tori Kelly - *Colors of the Wind*
Poetry: Jane Hirshfield - *On the Fifth Day*
         Toni Morrison - *It Comes Unadorned*

42

Treasure Map

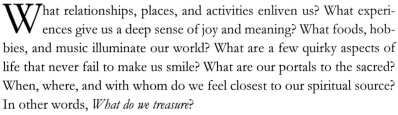

When we women offer our experience as our truth,
as human truth, all the maps change. ~Ursula K. LeGuin

What relationships, places, and activities enliven us? What experiences give us a deep sense of joy and meaning? What foods, hobbies, and music illuminate our world? What are a few quirky aspects of life that never fail to make us smile? What are our portals to the sacred? When, where, and with whom do we feel closest to our spiritual source? In other words, *What do we treasure?*

Sometimes we don't recognize that aspects of our lives we think of as optional, peripheral, or something we can do after all the other "important" things are done, are actually *essential* sources of our life satisfaction, wellness, and growth.

Positive psychology tells us it is often easier to focus on difficult aspects of our lives than on positive ones. Our friend Rick Hanson likes to say that our minds are like Velcro for the negative and Teflon for the positive. Paying attention to and *savoring* what brings us meaning and joy can build resilience and counteract stress and depression. It can also help us shift our priorities and make time for what we treasure.

Mapmaking is an imaginative tool for self-reflection. We make a treasure map of our lives in this activity, illustrating the life-enhancing places, people, interests, and activities that allow us to connect with our most creative, authentic selves. Whether we make a pirate's treasure map, a neighborhood street map, a map of a fantasy castle and surrounds, or a map of the body, we will use mostly pictures and few words to create our symbolic maps.

Materials

Large butcher or art paper; pens; scissors; colored markers and pencils, crayons; stickers, Washi tape; magazines with pictures and words to cut out

Step-by-Step Guidelines

- Assure members there is no "right way" to create a personal map—it can be linear, going from east to west or north to south, be enclosed by borders, or be circular. It can be a cartoon bubble chart or flowchart, and be chronological or not. There are no rules!

- Ask members to jot down four lists: places that inspire awe; people who have had a strong positive influence; hobbies or interests that enrich their lives; and specific activities that bring them joy.

- Play some music while members place items from their lists on their maps. Encourage them to use copious art materials. Go all out. Have fun!

- Allow time for volunteers to share their maps, in dyads or triads for larger groups.

Suggested Resources

Books: Jill K. Berry and Linden McNeilly - *Map Art Lab*
Rick Hanson - *Hardwiring Happiness: The New Brain Science of Contentment, Calm and Confidence*
Music: Kacey Musgraves - *Follow Your Arrow*
Natalie Merchant - *Motherland*
Luca Mundaca - *Ha Dias*
MaMuse - *Hallelujah*
Online: Search Google Images for "Personal Art Maps"

43

Exploring the Four Addictions

If your desire feels wrong to you: Go deeper. ~Glennon Doyle

Angeles Arrien wrote that from a cross-cultural perspective, there are four universal addictions or patterns to which all humans are susceptible. While we might not have an addiction to a substance or other harmful behavior, we can feel dependent on other things for our happiness.

If we have a low tolerance for boredom and crave excitement, we may develop an *addiction to intensity.* We tend to exaggerate our life experiences, be attracted to charismatic or troubled friends or romantic partners, create drama, or over-use substances or sex to feel more alive.

If we are *addicted to perfection,* we don't tolerate mistakes and view vulnerability as weakness. We are hard on others and ourselves. If we have to be perfect, it is difficult to be authentic.

If *addicted to the need to know,* we can become uncomfortable with life's surprises or things we don't understand. We may become controlling in relationships or thrown off when things don't turn out the way we'd planned.

We can also have the *addiction to being fixated on what is not working.* Our attention is frequently drawn to what could go wrong, we suspect the worst, and we tend to point out the flaws in people and situations. We may exaggerate our negative experiences or blow them out of proportion.

All of us are susceptible to developing these addictive patterns to deal with discomfort, disappointment, or feelings of emptiness in our lives. This activity lets us explore our addictive patterns with honesty and self-compassion.

Materials

Copies of the activity description for each member (or write the four patterns and their definitions on a whiteboard or flipchart)

Step-by-Step Guidelines

- Read the activity description and ask members to reflect in silence for a few minutes.
- Ask members to focus on the pattern(s) they most clearly recognize in themselves. If they are not sure, they can ask themselves what a close friend or family member might say about them if asked.
- Break into dyads and ask members to take turns responding to these questions, one at a time. Allow about five minutes for each person to respond to each question, taking ten minutes for each question, thirty minutes in total.
  o *Of the four addictions, which is most expressed in me, and in what ways?*
  o *How has this pattern affected my intimate relationships?*
  o *How has this pattern affected my life in general—in work, as a parent, as a friend?*
- Return to the circle and ask if any members would like to share the pattern they identified.
- Ask members to reflect on how they will notice and experiment with the opposite of their pattern in the coming week. For example, those with an addiction to intensity might explore savoring boredom, or those who need to know could explore living in "the land of I don't know."

Suggested Resources

Book: Angeles Arrien - *The Four-Fold Way: Walking the Paths of the Warrior, Teacher, Healer, and Visionary*
Music: Kelly Clarkson - *Stronger*
        Beautiful Chorus - *I Am*
        Woven Kin, Leah Song - *Down Deeper*

44

Spirit Dolls

If you have wisdom, let others light their candles in it. ~Margaret Fuller

This activity requires more materials and time than most.
Saving it for a retreat day is ideal.

Spirit dolls have been used in rites of passage, in meaningful celebrations, and for healing for thousands of years. In Pueblo Indian culture, kachina dolls and masks represent animals, forces of nature, spirit beings, or ancestors; they serve as a bridge between the spirit world and mortals. Spirit dolls are also found among the African Diaspora traditions, such as Santeria. They represent spirits or divine beings (called Orishas), for example, Yemaya—the goddess of the ocean, family, love, fertility, and home.

Spirit dolls are not toys; they are spirit-infused objects that can bring our inner wisdom and vision forward. Repressed aspects of our personality, spirituality, and sensuality may come into the light. Making spirit dolls in group rituals is an empowering path to deeper levels of connection with nature, close friends, and loved ones.

It is important to know there is no right or wrong way to create a spirit doll; it's not about the prettiest or most elaborate doll. The activity focuses on gaining insight, courage, or self-knowledge, or on simply experiencing the joy we feel from being creative and open to any entity or symbolic essence our spirit doll brings forward.

Materials

Sticks; cotton or batting; glue guns; fabric scraps; twine or thread; buttons, shells, feathers, old jewelry, ribbons, yarns

Step-by-Step Guidelines

- Before the meeting, share the activity description with members, and ask them to bring supplies they may want to work with. The group leader may bring supplies as well, including multiple options for the body of the dolls, such as sturdy sticks, pieces of bark, cardboard. If there is time and you are meeting near nature, ask members to take a walk and gather sticks, cones, stones, feathers, etc.

- Ask each member to set an intention for her doll—perhaps to honor a friend or ancestor, represent an animal or divine spirit, or to embody an aspect of herself (such as the wild woman, the healer, or the crone).

- Whether the doll is simple or elaborate, she (or he if a male appears) will carry the energy of her maker's intention. *Discourage over-planning*, letting members' intuition allow their doll to develop spontaneously.

- Play music while everyone uses the above materials to make and embellish her doll with whatever calls to her. Listen for the doll's name; it will come. Remind members to focus on their own doll; this is not a competitive event!

- Allow time for everyone to introduce her doll to the group, saying her name (perhaps saying *I am she/he who* _____), and share her significance with the group.

Suggested Resources

Music: David and Steve Gordon - *Enter the Sacred*
El-Buho, Aluna Project - *Amalia*
Ashana & Thomas Barquee - *Soulmerge*
Poetry: rupi kaur - *you are more than beautiful*
May Sarton - *When a Woman Feels Alone*
Online: Search for Joanna P. Colbert's online how-to booklet *How to Make a Spirit Doll*

45

Releasing Ceremony

Letting go helps us to live in a more peaceful state of mind and helps restore our balance. It allows others to be responsible for themselves and for us to take our hands off situations that do not belong to us. This frees us from unnecessary stress.
~Melody Beattie

For centuries, people have used fire rituals and smoke to symbolically release unwanted energies and attachments from the past. When we are ready to let go of resentments, regrets, or outdated patterns, a burning ritual can allow us to release what no longer serves us and focus on new beginnings. It can also help with ending a relationship or detaching from someone to whom we have an unhealthy attachment.

Rituals or ceremonies are ways to express our intentions through symbolic objects and actions. When we want to emphasize or amplify our desire, in this case to release something that has been weighing us down, we can take symbolic actions in the real world that facilitate that inner work. They are used across cultures, in nearly every religious and spiritual tradition, and in secular contexts. Science shows that rituals work*, reducing anxiety and grief after loss.

A burning ceremony can help us to get unstuck, feel a sense of closure, and move on. It can be surprisingly helpful to see what we've been carrying around for so long go up in smoke. In this activity, we name what we want to release and set intentions for the future.

Materials

Personal journals; slips of paper and pens; a deep unburnable bowl or container suitable for safely burning papers, or a fire pit; a lighter; enough water to put out the fire

Step-by-Step Guidelines

- Share the activity description.
- Ask members to focus on what they would like to release for several minutes, either in silence or while you play meditative music.
- Ask them to write down what they want to release on a slip of paper. They can write a word, a name, an old ego wound, or an unhealthy thought pattern—perhaps lingering feelings of fear, anxiety, or sadness.
- Light a fire in a *safe* container like a deep cast iron or stone bowl, metal container, or outdoor fire pit (our favorite).

- Ask members to stand in a circle around the fire. One by one, ask them to drop their paper into the fire and visualize the unwanted thoughts or conditions being released as the smoke rises. If they want to, they can name what they are releasing aloud, for example *I am releasing _____, making room for more peace and joy in my life.*
- If a bowl or container is used, members can scatter the ashes into the wind or bury them after all the papers have been burned and cooled.

Suggested Resources

Music: Tina Turner - *Purity of Mind: Lotus Sutra*
 Pentatonix - *Let It Go*
 Rising Appalachia - *I Shall Be Released*
Poetry: Naomi Shahib Nye - *Burning the Old Year*
 Wendell Berry - *The Peace of Wild Things*

46

Quieting Perfectionism

Understanding the difference between healthy striving and perfectionism is critical to laying down the shield and picking up your life. Research shows that perfectionism hampers success. In fact, it's often the path to depression, anxiety, addiction, and life paralysis. ~Brené Brown

Women tend to set unrealistic expectations for themselves. We attempt to juggle work, parenting, health, appearance, and relationships without dropping any balls, and when we do fall short, we believe that being hard on ourselves will help. We allow perfection to be the enemy of "good enough." Or we avoid pushing beyond our comfort zone because we don't want to fail, look silly, or make a mistake. We lower the bar and don't take risks because we can't do something perfectly. Both are forms of perfectionism.

Without realizing it, we can spend decades trying to live up to real or imaginary *shoulds* from society, our family, or our culture, allowing our authentic interests to languish. A self-critical voice in our minds can become dominant, like an internal bully. We believe the lie that if we are kinder to ourselves, we will not accomplish anything.

There is a difference between perfection and excellence. Perfection doesn't tolerate mistakes, while excellence learns from mistakes. What might happen if we quieted the inner perfectionist? We could strive for good most of the time and remember that excellence is born by learning from thousands of mistakes.

What would happen if our definition of good was *Better than yesterday?* What would happen if we said with joy, *I am practicing imperfection!* We could embrace the truth that being imperfect is the nature of being human: in fact, it is the nature of reality. As the tech folks say, it is a feature, not a bug.

In our women's circles, we have the space to try new things, to falter, and to try again. This activity invites us to practice another way to respond to our mistakes, and to turn down the volume of our perfectionist self-critic.

Materials

Personal journals or paper and pens

Step-by-Step Guidelines

- Read the activity description.
- Go around the circle or break into small groups and ask people to share ways that harsh self-criticism has held them back from making changes or pursuing dreams.
- Then, members write down three times in their lives when falling short or making a mistake ended up being a positive turning point for them. Examples might be "failing" in a way that paved the way for future success, such as getting fired from a job, and because of that, finding work that was much more satisfying, or learning from a period of burnout to prioritize self-care.
- Ask members to share these in dyads or triads with one another.
- Finally, ask members to share one thing they will commit to purposely performing imperfectly with a goal of "good enough" in the coming week (dancing, drawing, cooking, running, playing an instrument, playing golf—it can be anything). Ask women to see if they can enjoy and even revel in their mistakes, knowing that just giving it a try was a success.

Suggested Resources

Book: Brené Brown - *The Gifts of Imperfection: Let Go of Who You Think You're Supposed to Be and Embrace Who You Are*

Music: Libana - *I Will Be Gentle With Myself*
Joss Stone - *Right to Be Wrong*
Cheryl Wheeler - *Unworthy*

Poetry: Danna Faulds - *Awakening Now*

47

Beading Bracelets

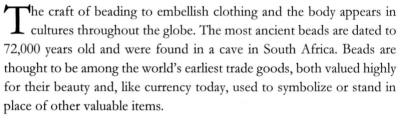

We are all beads strung together on the same thread of love.
~Mata Amritanandamayi

The craft of beading to embellish clothing and the body appears in cultures throughout the globe. The most ancient beads are dated to 72,000 years old and were found in a cave in South Africa. Beads are thought to be among the world's earliest trade goods, both valued highly for their beauty and, like currency today, used to symbolize or stand in place of other valuable items.

Beads have often been used ceremonially, including for prayer or contemplation, like the rosary in Catholicism or mala beads in Buddhism. Women throughout millennia have collectively beaded to offer blessings for a life passage like childbirth, coming of age, marriage, or death. Beaded items can serve as talismans, for protection or good luck, and can signify value, importance, honor, or respect. Beads can be worn as reminders of our intentions, of our culture and identity, or that we are loved.

In this activity, we imbue beads with blessings to celebrate the birth of a baby, a member's new job or new home, to offer support for an upcoming surgery, for healing from trauma, or a special birthday. Women can all bead one bracelet for a group member, giving her a powerful talisman to take into her life. For example, a mother-to-be can keep the bracelet near her during pregnancy and labor to remind her of the circle's support (and can later use it to remember from which breast she most recently fed the baby!). Or each member can bead their own bracelet to commemorate a significant occasion in her life, or simply to remind her of her intentions.

Materials

Small containers or egg cartons to hold beads; a variety of beads, both unique and "filler," (from craft, thrift, and dollar stores); stretchy cord for beading (such as Stretch Magic)

Step-by-Step Guidelines

- Before your meeting, ask members to bring a special bead that has meaning or significance, or one from an old piece of jewelry or found in a thrift shop or craft store.

- At the meeting, the beads can be strung into a bracelet for one member's special occasion (double or triple the bracelet for larger groups). Or each member can bead their own bracelet.

- If making a bracelet for one member, knot the end with a large anchor bead and pass the beading cord around. Each member will string one bead as they share a prayer, a thought, or a wish for an upcoming birth or another rite of passage. If women are making their own bracelets, they can add an intention or blessing to each bead as they string them one by one.

- After a few minutes of silence, offer an overall blessing, such as *May all of these or better come to pass*, and tie the bracelet ends together. Secure the knot and place the bracelet on the woman's wrist.

- If women are making their own bracelets, the completed bracelets can be passed around the group in a clockwise fashion for each member to embed their support and positive intentions into each bracelet.

Suggested Resources

Book: Cecilia Leibovitz - *Bead Jewelry Making for Beginners: Step-by-Step Instructions for Beautiful Designs*

Music: Sister Sledge - *We Are Family*
Sweet Honey in the Rock - *Somebody Prayed for Me*
Alexa Sunshine Rose - *Mother of the Water*

Online: Search YouTube for "easy beaded stretch cord bracelet"

48

I See You

*Being safe is about being seen and heard and allowed
to be who you are and to speak your truth.* ~Rachel Naomi Remen

*S*awubona is a Zulu greeting that means, literally, "I see you." A multilayered word, it includes *you are important to me, I value you, all of my attention is with you, I accept your strengths, your flaws, your fears, and your uniqueness.*

Being seen in this way is a gift. Too often, women can feel invisible, or defined by others' expectations. Or people see only the parts of us they want to see. To see other women, to pay attention to them with curiosity and kindness, welcoming *all* that they are, is an act of profound generosity and love.

In our everyday lives, it can be difficult to share with our partners, friends, coworkers, and family members how much we appreciate them. Being present with them, with kind attention and without judgment, is a simple way to do this.

Participating in an ongoing women's group lets us truly see one another. This simple activity gives us a way to express love and recognition for the women in our group, and to practice giving and receiving attention and appreciation.

Materials

Personal journals or paper and pens; a typed list of the prompts below for each member

Step-by-Step Guidelines

- Ask members to break into dyads and face each other.
- Ask the member with the longest hair to go first as the speaker. Ask the listener to maintain silence and open her heart to being seen by the speaker.
- Ask the speaker to complete these sentences aloud to their partner.
    - *What I've learned from you is . . .*
    - *What I honor and respect about you is . . .*
    - *What I love about you is . . .*
    - *What I want to know more about you is . . .*
- Ask the speaker and listener to switch places and repeat the process. If time allows, repeat the process with different dyads until many or all women have shared with one another.
- Allow time for members to journal about what they learned from this activity.
- Bring the circle back together and ask volunteers to share what they experienced during the activity.

Suggested Resources

Book: Marilyn Schiltz, Cassandra Vieten, Tina Amorok - *Living Deeply: The Art and Science Transformation in Everyday Life* (Chapter One: Seeing with New Eyes)

Music: Bruno Mars - *Just the Way You Are*
Sara Bareilles - *Brave*
Elaine Silver - *How Could Anyone*, from the album *Faerie Goddess*

Poetry: Lucille Clifton - *Good Woman* (book)
Jeanette LeBlanc - *I See You*

49

Superpowers

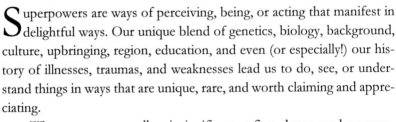

As women, we have superpowers. We are sisters. We are healers. We are mothers. We are goddess warriors. ~Merle Dandridge

Superpowers are ways of perceiving, being, or acting that manifest in delightful ways. Our unique blend of genetics, biology, background, culture, upbringing, region, education, and even (or especially!) our history of illnesses, traumas, and weaknesses lead us to do, see, or understand things in ways that are unique, rare, and worth claiming and appreciating.

What may seem small or insignificant at first glance can be a powerful gift. We may be able to recommend the perfect book for someone or bake the ultimate loaf of sourdough bread. Maybe we have a special capacity to listen carefully and hear what people are *not* saying, lift others up, or invent solutions to intractable problems. It might be the ability to recognize patterns in data, perform surgery, design websites, or create multinational collaborative networks for the public good.

Neurodiversity celebrates the wide variety of ways our brains are wired, as opposed to labeling some things as "abnormal" and some as "normal." Research shows that limited abilities in one arena can be accompanied by extraordinary abilities in another. For example, Temple Grandin writes and speaks about her autism. While it limited her intuitive understanding of how to interact with people, she could understand animal perspectives so completely that her designs revolutionized how cattle were slaughtered, making the process more humane.

We all have our zones of genius. In this activity, we will reflect on our superpowers, investigate and celebrate them, and share them with the group.

Materials

Journal and paper or pens

Step-by-Step Guidelines

- Ask members to write short answers to the following questions. Read the questions one at a time, giving members a couple of minutes to write their answers.

    o *What comes naturally to you?*
    o *What fills you with passion?*
    o *What makes time disappear for you?*
    o *What makes you different or weird?*
    o *About what do your friends ask advice?*
    o *What did you love to do as a child?*
    o *What would you do if money didn't matter?*

- Ask members to reflect on what answers keep appearing.
- Allow time for members to share what they learned with the group, and discuss ways they can acknowledge, celebrate, and boost their superpower.
- Follow by playing music and encouraging celebratory dancing!

Suggested Resources

Book: Jenara Nerenberg - *Divergent Mind: Thriving in a World that Wasn't Meant for You*

Music: Alicia Keys - *Superwoman*
Aretha Franklin/ Eurythmics - *Sisters Are Doing It for Themselves*
Katy Perry - *Roar*

* Dr. Michelle Millis Chappel (www.michellechappel.com), who has a Ph.D. in psychology from Princeton and was voted "Most Inspirational Professor" at the University of California, Santa Cruz, developed the questions in this activity. Despite being called "crazy" by a few colleagues, she ditched academics to follow her dream to be a rock star and has since won 17 Billboard International Songwriting awards.

50

Our Mothers

If it's not one thing, it's your mother. ~Robin Williams

Mother-daughter relationships are often complex. Whether fraught with conflict, or a strong, warm, and loving connection, our experiences with our mother can influence how we feel about ourselves, how we relate to others, how we parent or serve as maternal figures, how we interact with women in authority positions or how we behave as leaders, and much more. As we age, our mothers can show up in the mirror, in our families, in our therapy sessions, in our fashion, our self-care, our mental chatter . . . and so on.

Cultural messages about mothers affect us as well. In some cultures, a mother should be self-sacrificing, put her own needs and dreams aside, and serve her (particularly male) counterparts, parents, bosses, and children. In others, mothers hold the power, make the tough decisions, run the household, and are the warriors. In modern times, mothers are often expected to (and many want to) care for the family and the household as well as achieve a successful career. In some families mothers are revered and respected, and in others, they are diminished and controlled. It is important to realize that our mothers did not develop in a vacuum, but in a context of cultural expectations and values.

In women's groups, diving into this core relationship can be enlightening. Talking about our mothers and who they are (or were) helps us to connect more deeply with them or differentiate from them if we need to (or both!). It can help us clarify who we are and want to be as mothers ourselves, whether of our own children or as mother figures to others. We talk about our mothers in this activity, and how our experience with them impacts our lives today.

Materials

A place of honor or altar where women can put photos of their mothers/maternal figures

Step-by-Step Guidelines

- Before your meeting, ask members to bring a picture of their mother or another maternal figure to be placed on the altar.

- After opening the circle, ask each woman to hold her mother's picture and introduce her by name to the circle. Remind women to be especially attentive to shared agreements during this session (listening non-judgmentally, refraining from advice-giving, asking permission to inquire further, confidentiality) since this can be a sensitive topic for many.

- Lead a discussion in two parts. First, give each woman the opportunity to share memories of her mother as she grew up. If the group is large, break up into dyads or triads. To encourage the sharing, some possible questions are:
  - *What are three adjectives you would use to describe your mother when you were growing up?*
  - *What was one thing you were in sync with your mother about growing up, and one thing you were on different wavelengths about?*

- In a second round of sharing bring the discussion into the present, in small groups if necessary.
  - *How did your mother change over your lifetime?*
  - *Which of your mother's traits do you see in yourself?*
  - *How would you describe your relationship now, even if your mother has passed?*
  - *What might you need to resolve, let go of, or come to peace with around your mother?*

Suggested Resources

Book: Maya Angelou - *Mom and Me and Mom*
Music: Oumou Sangare - *Iyo Djeli*
        Tina Turner - *Mother Within*
        Windsong Dianne Martin - *Mother I Feel You*
        Little Big Town - *The Daughters*
        Robert Gass - *Ancient Mother*
Poetry: rupi kaur - *i will have to wait 'till i'm a mother*

51

What Is a Woman?

*Do not live someone else's life and someone else's idea of
what womanhood is. Womanhood is you.* ~Viola Davis

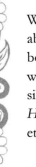

What does it mean to be a woman? While stereotypes of femininity
abound (passive, receptive, pretty, maiden, mother, whore, virgin, tom-
boy, cheerleader, wonder woman, bitch . . . the list goes on), the truth is
women are not any one of these things. From youth to old age, the pos-
sibilities of being a woman are limitless. In her 1949 book *Women Are
Here to Stay*, Agnes Rogers called us "the durable sex in its infinite variety." Yes, we are!

We can be playful, fierce, nurturing, wise, silly, angry, and loving,
sometimes all at once. We can be aggressive, petty, self-centered, and
two-faced. We can be strong and weak, brave, and cowardly, and everything in between. As the title of our book suggests, it's time to welcome
all that we are. It's like in the movie *Postcards from the Edge*, when Jack says
I don't like this particular side of you, to which Suzanne responds *I'm not a
box, I don't have sides! This is it, one side fits all!*

This activity explores the women we have known or learned about
who have influenced our definition of the feminine.

Materials

Personal journals or paper and pens; music and poetry

Step-by-Step Guidelines

- Read the activity description.
- Open the circle by sharing music and poetry about womanhood.
- Ask members to close their eyes and breathe deeply, counting backwards from 10 on each in-breath. Ask them to bring to mind women they have known or learned about that were important to them, have moved or inspired them, or that they admire. Encourage them to consider women across the spectrum—teachers, explorers, mothers, girls, elders. Ask them to purposely stretch their ideas of what kinds of women are inspiring. Remind them these may be women who made them feel uncomfortable as well.
- Ask members to make a list of the women that came up for them, next to their names, write responses to these questions:
  - *What do you admire about these women?*
  - *What about these women elicit discomfort in you?*
  - *What are your roles today?*
  - *What qualities do you want to model as a woman?*
  - *What are you hoping your role will be as you grow older?*
- Allow time for members to share some of their responses to the questions.

Suggested Resources

Books: Chimamanda Ngozi Adichie - *Dear Ijeawele, or a Feminist Manifesto in Fifteen Suggestions: We Should All Be Feminists*

Music: India.Arie - *Video*
Katy Perry - *What Makes a Woman*
The Highwomen - *Redesigning Woman*
Pretenders - *Hymn to Her*
May Erlewine - *Never One Thing*

Poetry: Maya Angelou - *Phenomenal Woman*
Amanda Lovelace - *Women Are Some Kind of Magic* book series

52

Spring Equinox

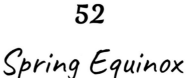

I want to stand by the river in my finest dress. I want to sing, strong and hard, and stomp my feet with a hundred others so that the waters hum with our happiness. I want to dance for the renewal of the world. ~Robin Wall Kimmerer

At the Spring Equinox, around March 21 in the Northern Hemisphere, the Earth is in perfect balance. The day and night are of equal length, and we are invited to welcome balance to our lives as well.

Spring is the season to plant the seeds for growth in our actual gardens and our metaphorical ones. It is a time for gently nurturing new ideas, some of which will gestate into full-fledged projects. New creative endeavors begin to take root within us. When the green stems of possibility emerge, we welcome their arrival.

It is a good time to celebrate renewal and rid our homes of the old: refresh the linens, rotate the art on the walls, clean out our closets, clear out our email inbox, redecorate our office, or replenish our pantries. We revel in warmer days, begin to feel more playful, and lift our faces to the sun. We move into the light and our spirits come alive. The darker months are over, and we can enjoy all the signs of life being reborn.

We honor the change in seasons with symbols and activities that represent new beginnings, like decorating eggs, planting seeds, gathering the first spring flowers, and celebrating the fertility of animals like bunnies and lambs. In Christian tradition, we celebrate the resurrection of Christ. Pre-dating this, Spring rituals around the world focused on fertility and birth, including celebrating the goddess of fertility, Eostre—hence the rabbits and eggs in today's Easter. This activity encourages us to revel in the colorful gifts and rites of spring,

Materials

Personal journals or paper and pens; colorful fabric; flowers, sprigs of greenery and other natural elements; dyed eggs; packets of flower seeds; goodies to share

Step-by-Step Guidelines

- Before your group meets, lay colorful fabric, seed packets, colorful eggs, and flowers on your altar or floor.
- Ask members to bring sweets to share along with items that represent spring to them, such as flowers, seeds, and pictures of newborn animals.
- At the meeting, ask members to add their items to the altar or floor. Spring's altar should be exuberant!
- Play music while members write about something new they want to bring into their life this spring. Writing prompts could be:
  - *What new ideas have been taking root in your mind over the winter?*
  - *What are you looking forward to doing with those ideas now?*
  - *What new experience would you like to have this spring?*
  - *How does your body feel as the warmer weather arrives?*
  - *What is a happy memory you have about springtime?*
- One by one, ask members to share their writing with the group.
- Celebrate the Spring Equinox with music and sweet treats.

Suggested Resources

Book: Robin Wall Kimmerer - *Braiding Sweetgrass: Indigenous Wisdom, Scientific Knowledge, and the Teachings of Plants*

Music: Nicola Cruz - *Levanta Muertos*
         Indigo Girls - *Southland in the Springtime*
         Lila - *Ladies Spin*
         Antonio Vivaldi - *Spring*

Poetry: Sappho - *Come to Me Here from Crete*
         Barbara Kingsolver - *Ephemera*

Women coming together is change.
Women staying together is power.
Women having each other's back
is the movement we need
now, then, and forever.
~ Soumya Mohanty Vilekar

Recommended Reading

Adichie, C. (2018). Dear Ijeawele, or A Feminist Manifesto in Fifteen Suggestions. Anchor. ISBN: 978-0525434801

Anders, C. (2016). All the Birds in the Sky. Tor Books. ISBN: 978-0765379948

Anderson, S. and Patricia Hopkins. (1992). The Feminine Face of God: The Unfolding of the Sacred in Women. Bantam Books. ISBN: 978-0553352665

Angelou, M. (2013). Mom and Me and Mom. Random House. ISBN: 978-1400066117

Angelou, M. (1978). And Still I Rise: A Book of Poems. Random House. ISBN: 978-0394502526

Arrien, A. (2007). The Second Half of Life: Opening the Eight Gates of Wisdom. Sounds True, Inc. ISBN: 978-1591795728

Arrien, A. (2000). The Nine Muses: A Mythological Path to Creativity. Jeremy P. Tarcher/Putnam. ISBN: 978-0874779998

Arrien, A. (1993). The Four-Fold Way: Walking the Paths of the Warrior, Teacher, Healer, and Visionary. Harper San Francisco. ISBN: 978-0062500597

Artress, L. (2006). Walking a Sacred Path: Rediscovering the Labyrinth as a Spiritual Practice. Riverhead Books. ISBN: 978-1594481819

Artress, L. (2006). The Sacred Path Companion: A Guide to Walking the Labyrinth to Heal and Transform. Riverhead Books. ISBN: 978-1594481826

Atwood, M. (1987). Selected Poems II (1976-1986). Mariner Books. ISBN: 978-0395454060

Baer, K. (2020). What Kind of Woman. Harper Perennial. ISBN: 978-0063008427

Baldwin, C. (1998). Calling the Circle: The First and Future Culture. Bantam Books. ISBN: 978-0553379006

Baldwin, C. & Linnea, A. (2010). The Circle Way: A Leader in Every Chair. Berrett-Koehler Publishers. ISBN: 978-1605092560

Baraz, J. (2012). Awakening Joy: 10 Steps to Happiness. Parallax Press. ISBN: 978-1937006228

Barnstone, W. (ed.). (2009). The Complete Poems of Sappho. Shambhala. ISBN: 978-1590306130

Barks, C., trans. (2004). The Essential Rumi. HarperOne. (Original work published 1997) ISBN: 978-9962599598

Bass, E. (2020). Indigo. Copper Canyon Press. ISBN: 978-1556595752

Belloni, A. (2019). Healing Journeys with the Black Madonna: Chants, Music, and Sacred Practices of the Great Goddess. Bear & Company. ISBN: 978-1591433422

Berry, Jill K. & McNeilly, L. (2014). Map Art Lab: 52 Exciting Art Explorations in Mapmaking, Imagination, and Travel. Quarry Books. ISBN: 978-1592539055

Berry, W. (1987). Collected Poems, 1957-1982. North Point Press. ISBN: 978-086547197

Bly, R. (1999). The Soul Is Here for Its Own Joy: Sacred Poems from Many Cultures. Ecco. ISBN: 978-0880014755

Bolen, J. S. (2014). Goddesses in Older Women: Archetypes in Women Over Fifty. Harper Paperbacks. (Original work published 2001) ISBN: 978-0060929237

Bolen, J. S. (2014). Goddesses in Everywoman: Powerful Archetypes in Women's Lives. Harper Paperbacks. (Original work published 1984) ISBN: 978-006232112

Bolen, J. S. (2003). Crones Don't Whine: Concentrated Wisdom for Juicy Women. Conari Press. ISBN: 978-1573249126

Bolen, J. S. (1999). The Millionth Circle: How to Change Ourselves and the World: The Essential Guide to Women's Circles. Conari Press. ISBN: 978-157324162

Bolen, J. S. (1994). Crossing to Avalon. HarperCollins Publisher. ISBN: 978-0062501127

Boorstein, S. (1997). It's Easier Than You Think: The Buddhist Way to Happiness. HarperOne. ISBN: 978-0062512949

Borysenko, J. (2001). Pocketful of Miracles: Prayer, Meditations, and Affirmations to Nurture Your Spirit Every Day of the Year. Grand Central Publishing. Amazon Kindle Edition.

Brown, B. (2010). The Gifts of Imperfection: Let Go of Who You Think You're Supposed To Be and Embrace Who You Are. Hazelden Publishing. ISBN: 978-1592858491

Brown, B. (2015). Daring Greatly: How the Courage To Be Vulnerable Transforms the Way We Live, Love, Parent, and Lead. Avery. ISBN: 978-1592408412

Buenaflor, E. (2021). Animal Medicine: A Curanderismo Guide to Shapeshifting, Journeying, and Connecting with Animal Allies. Bear and Company. Amazon Kindle Edition.

Cameron, J. (2016). The Artist's Way. 25th Anniversary Edition. TarcherPerigee. ISBN: 978-0143129257

Cameron, J. (2016). It's Never Too Late to Begin Again: Discovering Creativity and Meaning at Midlife and Beyond. TarcherPerigee. ISBN: 978-0399174216

Campbell, J. (2013). Goddesses: Mysteries of the Feminine Divine (Collected Works of Joseph Campbell). New World Library. ISBN: 978-1608681822

Campbell, J. (1991). The Power of Myth. Anchor. ISBN: 978-0385418867

Carnes, R. and Craig, S. (1998). Sacred Circles: A Guide to Creating Your Own Women's Spirituality Group. HarperOne. ISBN: 978-0062515223

Carroll, R. (2018). The Bullet Journal Method: Track the Past, Order the Present, Design the Future. Portfolio. ISBN: 978-0525522227

Chapman, S. G. (2012). The Five Keys to Mindful Communication: Using Deep Listening and Mindful Speech to Strengthen Relationships, Heal Conflicts, and Accomplish Your Goals. Shambhala. ISBN: 978-1590309414

Chappel, M. Create a Life That Totally Rocks: A Creative Path to Your Superpowers and Purpose. Forthcoming Book

Chittister, J. (2006) The Friendship of Women: The Hidden Tradition of the Bible. BlueBridge. ISBN: 978-1933346021

Chodron, P. (2018) The Places That Scare You: A Guide to Fearlessness in Difficult Times. Shambhala. ISBN: 978-1611805963

Chodron, P. (2016). When Things Fall Apart: Heart Advice for Difficult Times. Shambhala. ISBN: 978-1511803438

Chopra, Mallika (2015). Living With Intent: My Somewhat Messy Journey to Purpose, Peace and Joy. Harmony. ISBN: 978-0804139878

Chopra, Deepak (2020). Total Meditation: Practices in Living the Awakened Life. Harmony. ISBN: 978-1984887993

Christ, C. (1995). Diving Deep and Surfacing: Women Writers on Spiritual Quest. Beacon Press. ISBN: 978-0807062074

Clifton, L. (2000). Blessing the Boats: New and Selected Poems 1988-2000. BOA Editions Ltd. ISBN: 978-18880238882

Clifton, L. (1987). Good Woman: Poems and a Memoir 1969-1980. BOA Editions Ltd. ISBN: 978-0918526595

Colbert, J. (2012). How to Make a Spirit Doll. (Free online booklet) Joanna Powell Colbert Artworks.

Cornell, J. (2006). Mandala: Luminous Symbols for Healing. Quest Books. ISBN: 978-0835608473

Dass, R. (2001). Still Here: Embracing Aging, Changing, and Dying. Riverhead Books. ISBN: 978-15732228718

Cryar-DeBrucke, Z. (2016). Your Inner GPS: Follow Your Internal Guidance to Optimal Health, Happiness, and Satisfaction. New World Library. ISBN: 978-1608684120

Dillard, A. (1998). Holy the Firm. Harper Perennial. ISBN: 978-0060915438

Domar, A. and Dreher, H. (1999). Self-Nurture: Learning to Care for Yourself as Effectively as You Care for Everyone Else. Viking. ISBN: 978- 0670882861

Doyle, G. (2020). Untamed. The Dial Press. ISBN: 978-1984801258

Earth Prayers: 365 Prayers, Poems, and Invocations from Around the World. Elizabeth Roberts and Elias Amidon, eds. (2009). HarperOne. ISBN: 978-0062507464

Estés, C. P. (1992). Women Who Run With the Wolves: Myths and Stories of the Wild Woman Archetype. Ballantine Books. ISBN: 978-0345377449

Eisler, R. (1988). The Chalice and the Blade: Our History, Our Future. HarperOne. ISBN: 978-0062502896

Encinias, J. (2021). Queen Owl Wings: A Collection of Poems. Jeannette Encinias. ISBN: 978-0578845418

Farmer, S. (2010). Earth Magic Oracle Cards: A 48-Card Deck and Guidebook. Hay House Inc. ISBN: 978-1401925352

Faulds, D. (2002). Go In and In: Poems From the Heart of Yoga. Peaceable Kingdom Books. ISBN: 978-0974410609

Fox, J. (1997). Poetic Medicine: The Healing Art of Poem-Making. Jeremy P. Tarcher/Putnam ISBN: 978-0874778823

Fox, J. (1995). Finding What You Didn't Lose: Expressing Your Truth and Creativity Through Poem-Making. Jeremy P. Tarcher/Putnam. ISBN: 978-0874778090

Freeman, M. (2000). Kindling the Celtic Spirit: Ancient Traditions to Illumine Your Life Throughout the Seasons. HarperOne. ISBN: 978-006251655

Frost, S. (2010). Soul Collage Evolving: An Intuitive Collage Process for Self-Discovery and Community. Hanford Mead Publishers. ISBN: 978-1592750214

Gawain, S. (2016) Creative Visualization: Use the Power of Your Imagination to Create What You Want in Your Life. New World Library. ISBN: 978-1608684644

Gay, R. (2019). The Book of Delights. Algonquin Books. ISBN: 1616207922

Gbowee, L. (2011). Mighty Be Our Powers: How Sisterhood, Prayer, and Sex Changed a Nation at War. Beast Books. ISBN: 978-0984295159

Gilbert, E. (2016). Big Magic: Creative Living Beyond Fear. Penguin Publishing Group. ISBN: 978-1594634727

Gill, N. (2021). Where Hope Comes From: Poems of Resilience, Healing, and Light. Hachette Books. ISBN: 978-0306826405

Goldberg, N. (2021). Writing Down the Bones Deck: 60 Cards to Free the Writer Within. Shambhala. ISBN: 978-1611809008

Goldberg, N. (2016). Writing Down the Bones: Freeing the Writer Within. Shambhala. ISBN: 978-1611803082

Gorman, A. (2021). The Hill We Climb and Other Poems. Viking. ISBN: 978-0060776732

Hafiz. (1999). The Gift. Penguin Compass. ISBN: 978-0140195811

Halifax, J. (2018). Standing at the Edge: Finding Freedom Where Fear and Courage Meet. Flatiron Books. ISBN: 978-1250101358

Hall, N. (2019). Those Women. Spring Publications. ISBN: 978-0882140711

Hanson, R. (2013). Hardwiring Happiness: The New Brain Science of Contentment, Calm, and Confidence. Harmony. ISBN: 978-0385347310

Hanson, R. (2020). Resilient: How to Grow an Unshakable Core of Calm, Strength, and Happiness. Harmony. ISBN: 978-0451498861

Harjo, J. (2021). Poet Warrior: A Memoir. W.W. Norton & Company. ISBN: 978-0393248524

Harjo, J. (2020). When the Light of the World Was Subdued, Our Songs Came Through: A Norton Anthology of Native Nations Poetry. W.W. Norton & Company. ISBN: 978-03933556809

Harjo, J. (2008). She Had Some Horses. W.W. Norton & Company. ISBN: 978-0393334210

Hart, M., J. Stevens, F. Lieberman. (1990). Drumming at the Edge of Magic: A Journey into the Spirit of Percussion. Harper San Francisco. ISBN: 978-0062503749

Hauntie (May Yang). (2017). To Whitey & the Cracker Jack. Anhinga Press. ISBN: 978-1934695531

Hershfield, J. (2021). Ledger. Knopf. ISBN: 978-1524711719

Hillman, A. (2016). Awakening the Energies of Love: Discovering Fire for the Second Time. Bramble Books. ISBN: 978-1883647230

Hirschi, G. (2016). Mudras: Yoga in Your Hands. Red Wheel/Weiser. ISBN: 978-1578631391

Houston, J. (1997). The Search for the Beloved: Journeys in Mythology and Sacred Psychology. TarcherPerigee. ISBN: 978-0874778717

Houston, J. (1997). The Possible Human: A Course in Extending Your Physical, Mental, and Creative Abilities. TarcherPerigee. ISBN: 978-0874778724

Irby, S. (2020). Wow, No Thank You: Essays. Vintage. ISBN: 978-0525563488

Jain, S. (2021). Healing Ourselves: Biofield Science and the Future of Health. Sounds True. ISBN: 978-1683644330

Johnson, R. (2017). Inner Gold: Understanding Psychological Projection. Chiron Publishing. ISBN: 978-1630514631

Ju, C. (2021). Under Clouds and City Lights: Poems and Illustrations. New Degree Press. ISBN: 978-1636769639

Jung, C. (1968). Man and His Symbols. Dell. ISBN: 978-0440351832

Jung, C. (1963). Memories, Dreams, Reflections. Pantheon. ISBN: 978-0394435800

Kaur, R. (2015). Milk and Honey. Andrews McMeel Publishing. ISBN: 978-1449474256

Kennedy, C. (2011). She Walks in Beauty: A Woman's Journey through Poems. Hyperion. ISBN: 978-1401341459

Kidd, S. (2016). The Dance of the Dissident Daughter: A Woman's Journey from Christian Tradition to the Sacred Feminine. HarperOne. ISBN: 978-0062573025

Kimmerer, R. (2015). Braiding Sweetgrass: Indigenous Wisdom, Scientific Knowledge, and the Teachings of Plants. Milkweed Editions. ISBN: 978-1571313560

Kingsolver, B. (2020). How To Fly (In Ten Thousand Easy Lessons). Harper Collins. ISBN: 978-0062993083

LaPorte, D. (2012). The Fire Starter Sessions: A Soulful + Practical Guide to Creating Success on Your Own Terms. Harmony. ISBN: 978-0307952103

LaMott, A. (2005). Plan B: Further Thoughts on Faith. Riverhead Books. ISBN: 978-1573222990

LaMott, A. (1995). Bird by Bird: Some Instructions on Writing and Life. Anchor. ISBN: 978-0385480017

Lea, S., ed. (2004). The Breath of Parted Lips: Voices from The Robert Frost Place, Vol. II. CavanKerry Press. ISBN: 978-0967885681

Leibovitz, C. (2019). Bead Jewelry Making for Beginners: Step-by-Step Instructions for Beautiful Designs. Rockridge Press. ISBN: 978-1641526425

Le Guin, U. K. (2020). So Far So Good. Copper Canyon Press. ISBN: 978-1556596124

Light, A. (2015). Iron Spring. Airlie Press. ISBN: 978-0982106679

Lindbergh, A. (1991). Gift from the Sea. Pantheon. ISBN: 978-0679406839

Logan, M. (2020). Self-Love Workbook for Women: Release Self-Doubt, Build Self-Compassion, and Embrace Who You Are. Rockridge Press; Workbook Edition. ISBN: 978-1647397296

Lohmann, J. (2003). The Light of Invisible Bodies: Poems. Daniel and Daniel Publishing. ISBN: 978-1564744265

Lorde, A. (2000). The Collected Poem of Audre Lorde. W.W. Norton and Company. ISBN: 978-0393319729

Louden, J. (2020). Why Bother: Discover the Desire for What's Next. ISBN: 978-1989603123

Louden, J. (2007). The Life Organizer: A Woman's Guide to a Mindful Year. New World Library. ISBN: 978-1577315544

Louden, J. (2005). The Woman's Retreat Book. HarperOne. ISBN: 978-060776732

Lovelace, A. (2019). Women Are Some Kind of Magic (boxed set). Andrews McMeel Publishing. ISBN: 978-1524851453

Lowell, C. (2018). Meditative Mandala Making. A Grounding Practice to Nourish Your Soul. Amazon Kindle Edition.

Luke, H. (1984). Woman Earth and Spirit: The Feminine in Symbol and Myth. The Crossroad Publishing Co. ISBN: 978-0824506339

Machado, A. (1983). Times Alone: Selected Poems of Antonio Machado. Wesleyan University Press. ISBN: 978-0819560810

MantraCraft. (2019). 100 Mandalas: Stress Relieving Mandala Designs for Adults Relaxation. New Castle P&P. ISBN: 978-1945710346

Medicine Eagle, B. (1991). Buffalo Woman Comes Singing: The Spirit Song of a Rainbow Medicine Woman. Ballantine Books. ISBN: 978-03453361431

Mitchell, S. (1993). The Enlightened Heart: An Anthology of Sacred Poetry. Harper Perennial. ISBN: 978-0060920531

Mucklow, L. (2015). Portable Color Me Calm: 70 Coloring Templates for Meditation and Relaxation (A Zen Coloring Book). Race Point Publishing. ISBN: 978-16310061868

Mueller, L. (1996). Alive Together: New and Selected Poems. LSU Press. ISBN: 978-0807121283

Murdock, M. (2020). The Heroine's Journey: Woman's Quest for Wholeness. Shambhala. ISBN: 978-1611808308

Murdock, M. (2020). The Heroine's Journey Workbook: A Map for Every Woman's Quest. Shambhala. ISBN: 978-1611808315

Neff, K. (2021). Fierce Self-Compassion: How Women Can Harness Kindness to Speak Up, Claim Their Power, and Thrive. Harper Wave. ISBN: 978-0062992065

Neff, K. and Germer, C. (2018). The Mindful Self-Compassion Workbook: A Proven Way to Accept Yourself, Build Inner Strength, and Thrive. Guilford Press. ISBN: 978-1462526789

Neilhardt, J. (2014). Black Elk Speaks: The Complete Edition. Bison Books. ISBN: 978-0803283916

Nepo, M. with J. Curtis. (2020). The Book of Awakening: Having the Life You Want by Being Present to the Life You Have. Red Wheel. (Original work published 2000) ISBN: 978-1590035009

Nepo, M. (2016). The Way Under the Way: The Place of True Meeting. Sounds True. ISBN: 978-1622037544

Nerenberg, J. (2020). Divergent Mind: Thriving in a World That Wasn't Designed for You. HarperOne. Amazon Kindle Edition.

Neruda, Pablo. (2004). The Essential Neruda: Selected Poems. City Lights Publishers. ISBN: 978-0872864283

Noble, V. (1994). Motherpeace: A Way to the Goddess Through Myth, Art, and Tarot. HarperOne. ISBN: 978-0062510853

Norton, J. and M. Starbird. (2009). 14 Steps to Awaken the Sacred Feminine: Women in the Circle of Mary Magdalene. Bear & Company. ISBN: 978-1591430919

O'Donohue, J. (2008). To Bless the Space Between Us: A Book of Blessings. Doubleday. ISBN: 978-0385522274

Oliver, M. (2019). Upstream: Selected Essays. Penguin Books. ISBN: 978-0143130086

Oliver, M. (2017). Devotions: The Selected Poems of Mary Oliver. Penguin Press. ISBN: 978-0399563249

Oliver, M. (2013). A Thousand Mornings: Poems. Penguin Books. ISBN: 978-0143124054

Oliver, M. (2009). Red Bird. Beacon Press. ISBN: 978-0807068939

Oliver, M. (2007). Thirst. Beacon Press. ISBN: 978-0807068977

Oliver, M. (2006) Owls and Other Fantasies: Poems and Essays. Beacon Press. ISBN: 978-0807068755

Oliver, M. (2004). New and Selected Poems, Volume One. Beacon Press. ISBN: 978-0807068779

Oliver, M. ((1986). Dream Work. The Atlantic Monthly Press. ISBN: 978-0871130693

Pennebaker, J. W., and Smyth, J. M. (2016). Opening Up by Writing It Down: How Expressive Writing Improves Health and Eases Emotional Pain. The Guilford Press. ISBN: 978-1462524921

Pipher, M. (2020). Women Rowing North: Navigating Life's Currents and Flourishing As We Age. Bloomsbury Publishing. ISBN: 978-1632869616

Pipher, M. and S. P. Gilliam. (2019). Reviving Ophelia 25th Anniversary Edition: Saving the Selves of Adolescent Girls. Riverhead Books. ISBN: 978-0525537045

Piercy, M. (1982). Circles on the Water. Alfred A. Knopf, Inc. Knopf. ISBN: 978-0394707792

Redmond, L. (2018). When the Drummers Were Women: A Spiritual History of Rhythm. Echo Point Books & Media. ISBN: 978-1635617887

Remen, R. (2006). Kitchen Table Wisdom: Stories That Heal (10th Anniversary Edition). Riverhead Books. ISBN: 978-1594482090

Remen, R. (2001). My Grandfather's Blessings: Stories of Strength, Refuge, and Belonging. Riverhead Books. ISBN: 978-1573228565

Rhimes. S. (2016). Year of Yes: How To Dance It Out, Stand in the Sun, and Be Your Own Person. Simon and Schuster. ISBN: 978-1476777122

Rich, A. and Gelpi, A. (eds.). (2018). Selected Poems: 1950-2012. W. W. Norton & Company. ISBN: 978-0393355116

Rilke, R. M. (1989). The Selected Poetry of Rainer Maria Rilke. Vintage. ISBN: 978-0679722014

Rogers, B. (2008). "The White Place" in Once Upon a Place: Writings from Ghost Ranch. Night Owl Books. ISBN: 978-0977115143

Ruiz, D. J. (2020). The Medicine Bag: Shamanic Rituals & Ceremonies for Personal Transformation. Hierophant Publishing. Amazon Kindle Edition.

Salzberg, S. (2003). Faith: Trusting Your Own Deepest Experience. Riverhead Books. ISBN: 978-1573222280

Salzberg, S. (2002). Lovingkindness: The Revolutionary Art of Happiness. Shambhala. ISBN: 978-1570629037

Sams, J. and Carson, D. (1988). Medicine Cards. Bear & Co. ISBN: 0-939680-53-X

Sarton, M. (1993). Collected Poems, 1930-1993. W. W. Norton & Company. ISBN: 978-0393034936

Schlitz, M., Cassandra Vieten, Tina Amorok. (2008). Living Deeply: The Art and Science of Transformation. New Harbinger/Noetic Books. ISBN: 978-1572245334

Shapiro, S. (2020). Good Morning, I Love You: Mindfulness and Self-Compassion Practices to Rewire Your Brain for Calm, Clarity, and Joy. Sounds True. ISBN: 978-1683643432

Shea, M. (2016). Kaleidoscope Mandala Coloring Book: 50 Mandala Designs for Stress Relief, Relaxation and Art Therapy. ISBN: 978-1532713217

Silvermarie, S. (2020). Poems for Flourishing. Independently Published. ISBN: 979-8650416012

Singer, M. (2007). The Untethered Soul: The Journey Beyond Yourself. New Harbinger Publications. ISBN: 978-157224372

Sisters of the Earth: Women's Prose and Poetry About Nature. Lorraine Anderson, ed. (2003). Vintage. ISBN: 978-140033218

Sobczak, C. (2014). Embody: Learning To Love Your Unique Body (and Quiet that Critical Voice). Gurze Books. ISBN: 978-1684424870

Stafford, W., and Kim Stafford, ed. (2014). Ask Me: 100 Essential Poems of William Stafford. Graywolf Press. ISBN: 978-1555976644

Stanley, J. (2017). Every Body Yoga: Let Go of Fear, Get On the Mat, Love Your Body. Workman Publishing Company. ISBN: 978-0761193111

Starhawk. (1994). The Fifth Sacred Thing. Bantam. ISBN: 978-0553373806

Starhawk. (1979). The Spiral Dance: A Rebirth of the Ancient Religion of the Great Goddess. Harper & Row. ISBN: 978-0676974676

Starr, M. (2019). Wild Mercy: Living the Fierce and Tender Wisdom of the Women Mystics. Sounds True. ISBN: 978-1683641568

Stewart, I. (2013). Sacred Woman, Sacred Dance. Inner Traditions. ISBN: 978-1620552506

Stone, M. (1990). Ancient Mirrors of Womanhood: A Treasury of Goddess and Heroine Lore from Around the World. Beacon Press. ISBN: 978-0807067512

Stone, M. (1978). When God Was a Woman. Mariner Books. ISBN: 978-0156961585

Svensson, H. (1995). The Runes. Barnes and Noble Books. ISBN 978-1842227442

Taylor. S. R. (2021). The Body Is Not an Apology, Second Edition: The Power of Radical Self-Love. Berrett-Koehler Publishers. ISBN: 978-1523090990

Teish, L. (2000). Jump Up: Good Times Throughout the Seasons With Celebrations from Around the World. Conari Press. ISBN: 978-1573245517

Teish, L. (1994). Carnival of the Spirit. Seasonal Celebrations and Rites of Passage. Apocryphile Press. ISBN: 978-1940671413

Teish, L. (1988). Jambalaya: The Natural Woman's Book of Personal Charms and Practical Rituals. HarperOne. ISBN: 978-0062508591

The Dalai Lama. (2020). The Art of Happiness: A Handbook for Living. Riverhead Books. ISBN: 978-1573227544

Tolle, E. (2008). A New Earth: Awakening to Your Life's Purpose. Penguin. ISBN: 978-0452289963

Tolle, E. (2004). The Power of Now: A Guide to Spiritual Enlightenment. New World Library. ISBN: 978-1577314806

Tribole, E. and E. Resch. (2017). The Intuitive Eating Workbook: Ten Principles for Nourishing Healthy Relationship with Food. New Harbinger. ISBN: 978-1626256224

Vaughan, F. (1979). Awakening Intuition. Anchor. ISBN: 978-0385133715

Vieten, C. (2009). Mindful Motherhood: Practical Tools for Staying Sane During Pregnancy and Your Child's First Year. New Harbinger Publications. ISBN: 978-1572246294

Whyte, D. (2012). River Flow: New & Selected Poems. Many Rivers Press. ISBN: 978-1932887280

Wilding, A. (2017). Wild & Wise: Sacred Feminine Meditations for Women's Circles & Personal Awakening. Womancraft Publishing. ISBN: 978-1910559376

Woodman, M. and Mellick, J. (2001). Coming Home to Myself: Reflections for Nurturing a Woman's Body and Soul. Conari Press. ISBN: 978-1573245661

Woodman, M. and Dickson, E. (1997). Dancing in the Flames: The Dark Goddess in the Transformation of Consciousness. Shambhala. ISBN: 978-1570623134

Woodman, M. (1982). Addiction to Perfection (Studies in Jungian Psychology). Inner City Books. ISBN: 978-0919123113

Woodman, M. (1980). The Owl Was a Baker's Daughter: Obesity, Anorexia Nervosa, and the Repressed Feminine: A Psychological Study. Inner City Books. ISBN: 978-0919123038

Visit our website!

www.watwabook.com

Billie Rogers, MA, MFT, has facilitated women's groups and retreats for 40 years. She remains passionate about life-long learning, passing on her mentors' gifts, counseling others seeking personal growth, and speaking up when a woman's voice must be heard. She was an Educational and Personal Counselor in Southern California for 25 years. She has taught Spanish and French, graduate school counseling classes, and language acquisition classes for international students. She attended and co-led two-year-long women's programs in the Transformational Arts, each ending with pilgrimages to holy sites in France. She has led volunteer service groups for many summers at a spiritual retreat center in Northern New Mexico. She writes, dabbles in gourd art and basket making, and travels extensively to women's sacred sites worldwide. Her essays, travel writing, and poetry have been published in anthologies, newsletters, and magazines.

Cassandra Vieten is a licensed clinical psychologist, a mind-body medicine researcher, an author, and an international workshop leader with nearly three decades of expertise in studying and teaching transformative experiences and practices. She has lead hundreds of women's groups, authored dozens of academic publications, as well as three books, including *Living Deeply: The Art and Science of Transformation in Everyday Life*, *Mindful Motherhood: Practical Tools for Staying Sane During Pregnancy and Your Child's First Year*, and *Spiritual and Religious Competencies in Clinical Practice: Guidelines for Psychologists and Mental Health Professionals*. She is Executive Director of the John W. Brick Mental Health Foundation, is a Research Scientist/Director of Research at the Arthur C. Clarke Center for Human Imagination at the University of California, San Diego, and has a small private practice in La Jolla, CA. She is a Senior Fellow at the Institute of Noetic Sciences, where she served for 18 years, the last six as IONS' seventh President. Cassandra is also a Psychology Today blogger, and her writing has been featured on Huffington Post. Learn more at cassandravieten.com.